THE FUNK & WAGNALLS

BOOK OF

PARLIAMENTARY PROCEDURE

THE FUNK & WAGNALLS BOOK

OF

Parliamentary Procedure

LAWRENCE WILFORD BRIDGE, A.M.

FUNK & WAGNALLS

Dedicated to
my wife
DONNA MORRISON BRIDGE

FUNK & WAGNALLS

A division of Reader's Digest Books, Inc.

PREFACE

PARLIAMENTARY LAW is the law governing the procedure in meetings of deliberative bodies. It is an accumulation of precedents, of regulations, and of principles adopted voluntarily by free men for the purpose of transacting business cooperatively in an efficient, expeditious, and democratic manner. It is a code of conduct and practice designed to assure rule by the majority and to prevent domination by minorities. At the same time it is a safeguard of minorities against possible tyranny of majorities. It is not an arbitrary standard; it is not the product of one mind; it is the considered judgment of generations of men, the product of gradual evolution through centuries of self-government, a contribution of enlightened society to the security and perpetuation of democracy. It may be altered by lawmaking bodies to meet complex legislative situations, but there is no radical departure from it. It may be supplemented locally by particular rules to meet special needs, or it may be modified by means of bylaws and constitutions adopted in accordance with its provisions. All matters of order not specifically provided for in bylaws and constitutions are customarily decided according to parliamentary law. Action that is unparliamentary is undemocratic and unenforceable, but an action that is strictly parliamentary has binding power and must be respected.

Parliamentary law is impartial, guaranteeing equal rights to all. It does not retard the transaction of business; on the contrary, it facilitates and expedites action. As the time-tested tool of experience, it provides a ready and efficient method for accomplishing all legitimate objectives of an assembly. It insists on orderly, systematic procedure, preventing confusion and misunderstanding. It demands unity of discussion, penalizing and instructing those who digress from the subject. It offers participation to all, imposes responsibilities on all, serves the best interests of all, and saves the time of all.

Despite these positive and unquestionable advantages, however, most meetings are conducted in a manner that is far from parliamentary, far from democratic. The fault is not that presiding officers are autocratic or that minorities deliberately try to usurp the place of power but that chairmen as a rule are unskilled, untutored, inexperienced and that laymen, the people who fill the seats in the assembly, are pitifully unaware of standard procedure, uninformed about their own rights and privileges, and undisciplined in the art of public discussion and cooperative behavior. The skills required for the successful conduct of meetings can be acquired under the instruction of competent teachers, but such teachers are scarce. They can be learned from trained parliamentarians, but such specialists are far from numerous. The only other source of help is a manual of parliamentary procedure.

There are, of course, numerous books on this subject, and these are available in libraries and bookstores, but many of these are far from simple. Some of them, in fact, themselves require an interpreter, being too exhaustive, too detailed, or too complicated to be of much use to the average person, who has but a vague knowledge of parliamentary rules beyond ordinary main motions. Other books are written by persons who, although they may be experts in the subject, apparently know little about readers. Still other texts deal largely with theory and strategy. Of what possible help are such books to a person who may understand nothing more than the bare rudiments of the subject? Surely the average layman is a beginner, and even many presiding officers are little more. If a book on parliamentary law is to render a service, it must be adapted to the multitude as well as to the expert.

Also such a book must do something more than tell the reader what to do; it must show him how to do it. Abstract directions must be supplemented by visual aids. A subject as difficult as parliamentary law must be made as concrete as possible by the use of practical, graphic devices. Even the expert would not be ungrateful for such help, and with it the novice will be encouraged. The present manual, embodying such instruction devices, is designed to accomplish the primary object of promoting intelligent, uninhibited, voluntary, general participation in discussion by the members of an organization and thus make them efficient and responsible members of a democratic society.

The reader's attention is called to the following features of this book:

1. The practical Table of Motions, with instructions for use. It is a compendium of standard parliamentary usage compressed into a few pages for quick reference.

2. The clear, concise exposition of parliamentary principles and rules of order, with abundant illustrations suitable for both expert and novice.

3. The sixteen charts and diagrams showing not only what should be done in certain situations but also how it should be done.

4. The numerous models for study, imitation, and guidance: model motions, resolutions, minutes, ballots, agenda, order of business, and models of six typical business meetings, giving the exact words of the chairman and speakers (46 pages).

5. The handy cross-references throughout the text.

6. The footnotes for details, exceptions, cautions, comments, minor points, etc., which in most books are not consistently differentiated from the main text and consequently result in confusion and obscurity.

7. The concise outline of a graded course of study for use by parliamentary law classes or clubs.

8. The detailed, comprehensive Index, facilitating reference to any special point.

9. This book is not a series of lectures or essays, as so many books are, even some that are called manuals. It is a real handbook, a genuine manual in the proper sense, a book for quick reference and easy study. All material is arranged in convenient outline form, showing logical coordination and proper subdivision of materials—the only proper form for a genuine manual.

This book has been in preparation for more than twelve years. It is the outgrowth of many years of teaching parliamentary law and public speaking. Much of it has been used in my classes, and all of it has developed from actual experience in practical problem solving. I have sought to make parliamentary law easier for all, not by altering standard practice or by omitting difficult motions and rules or by changing the familiar, conventional names of motions, but by clarifying meanings and procedures so that they will be intelligible to all. There is need, not of a new code of practice, but of a better understanding of the present code; not of revision, but of clearer exposition, better presentation, abler instruction. The subject, if it is to be mastered by the people who most need to know it, must be approached, not from the point of view of the legislator or expert or theorist, but from the point of view of the beginner, the laymen in the seats, or the common man who has been elevated to office. In this book it has been my purpose to demonstrate that these objectives can be attained without violating standard structure or sacrificing technical correctness.

L.W.B.

CONTENTS

THE FUNK & WAGNALLS

BOOK OF

PARLIAMENTARY PROCEDURE

THE TABLE OF MOTIONS

Instructions for use

NOTE: *The reader should not try to use the Table of Motions immediately following until he has studied the different kinds of motions—Main, Subsidiary, Privileged, Incidental, and Miscellaneous (pp. 21–46)—and the six Model Meetings (pp. 122–167).*

EACH MOTION listed in column (b) on the left side of the page has an identification number or letter in the immediately preceding column (a). The motions in the first group (Nos. 1–14), it will be noticed, are divided into three classes: Privileged Motions (Nos. 1–5), Subsidiary Motions (Nos. 6–13), and Main Motions (No. 14). Business is introduced by means of a Main Motion, which may be passed without change or may be modified or disposed of by application of one or more of the Subsidiary Motions listed above it. The TABLE enables the reader to tell at a glance what motions are permissible and what motions are "out of order" at any stage of the discussion.

The rank of each motion is indicated in column (d), and in the first group (Nos. 1–14) that rank happens to be the same as the identification number in column (a). In the second group (Nos. I–XII), where only two of these numbers appear in column (d); and in the third group (Letters A–N), where only one is used, they have the same meaning as in the first group: i.e., No. 14 indicates that the rank is that of a Main Motion, No. 10 that the rank is that of a motion "to commit or refer a main motion," and No. 12 shows that the motion is treated as an amendment.

The motion of the highest rank (No. 1) is at the top of the first group (Privileged Motions) and the one of lowest rank (No. 14) is the Main Motion; all others are ranked between these limits. No motion is "in order" if it is of lower rank than the pending motion, i.e., the motion that is being discussed. A motion "to amend" (No. 12) is out of order if a motion "to commit" (No. 10) is pending, and a motion "to commit" is out of order if made when a motion "to postpone to a certain time" (No. 9) has been made and is not yet disposed of. Any motion must yield to one of higher rank, i.e., to any motion indicated by a smaller number in column (a). Thus, all motions yield to No. 1; motions Nos. 3–14 inclusive, yield to

Nos. 2 or 1; motions Nos. 4–14 inclusive, yield to Nos. 3, 2, or 1; and so on.

A motion "to lay the question on the table" (No. 6) must be dealt with immediately, no matter how many other Subsidiary Motions have been made, for it takes precedence over all motions from No. 7 to No. 14 inclusive. However, any Privileged Motion (Nos. 1–5) will take precedence over a motion "to lay the question on the table." If a motion is made "to adjourn" (No. 2), no other motion is in order except "to fix the time to which to adjourn" (No. 1).

When a motion of any kind is pending, another motion of exactly the same kind is out of order. Thus a Main Motion must not be made while another Main Motion is being discussed. A motion "to amend" a certain question is out of order if another motion to amend the same question has been made and is not yet disposed of.

In the TABLE under Miscellaneous Motions and Incidental Motions the sequence as shown in column (a) means nothing at all about their rank or precedence. Miscellaneous Motions are identified by Roman numerals I to XII, and in column (d), in all instances except Nos. VIII and X, the rank is indicated by numerals as in Privileged, Subsidiary, and Main Motions. Nine of these motions are ranked as Main Motions (No. 14); one (No. VI) ranks as a motion "to commit" (No. 10); and one is marked MM, which, as explained in the Notes following the TABLE, means that it takes precedence over Main Motions.

Incidental Motions are identified by capital letters A to N in column (a) and in column (d) the rank or precedence is, with the single exception of Letter J, indicated by a special symbol explained in the Notes following the TABLE.

In all groups of the TABLE the numbers in column (j) harmonize with those in column (d) and with the foregoing explanations. In addition, I have shown in column (j) the Miscellaneous and Incidental Motions to which a given motion must yield. For example, a "Call for the Orders of the Day" (No. 5) must yield not only to the higher-ranking Privileged Motions (Nos. 1–4) but also to the Miscellaneous Motion "to reconsider" (No. VIII). A motion "to lay the question on the table" (No. 6) must give precedence to any Privileged Motion and to pending Incidental Motions. A motion "to amend an amendment" (No. 11) must yield precedence not only to all motions listed above it (Nos. 1–10) but also to all Incidental Motions, except F and G. And so on.

Special qualifications and restrictions of any given motion are indicated in column (c) by symbols explained in the Notes following the TABLE. There are six motions that have three or more symbols in column (c); two of these—the motions "to lay on the table" (No. 6) and "to reconsider" (No. VIII)—require close attention.

In the last column on the right (k) are listed the pages in the book on which will be found a detailed exposition of the corresponding motion. This is for quick use when there is not time to consult the Index or the analytic Table of Contents. The remaining columns are self-explanatory.

It would be desirable, of course, for a chairman to memorize the contents of the Table of Motions, but such an achievement would be phenomenal. The average—or even the exceptional—chairman needs to have this TABLE constantly in front of him while he is presiding. Moreover, he needs a competent secretary at his side to keep an accurate record of motions made and to assist him in all matters of uncertainty about their exact wording. Lay members of the club likewise would do well to have this manual at hand. By studying the rules and adhering strictly to them they can perform their required tasks; they will become appreciative, enlightened, functioning members of the assembly, and, by intelligent cooperation, they will be able to lighten the task of the chairman.

TABLE OF MOTIONS

(a) Identification	(b) RULES OF ORDER (For explanation of symbols, see pages 11–13.) See Note to Reader facing Chapter I for method of references to the Table in the text	(c) Qualifications or restrictions	(d) Rank or precedence	(e) Is it debatable?	(f) May it be amended?	(g) May it be reconsidered?	(h) Subsidiary motions applicable (besides Amend.)	(i) May it be renewed?	(j) Yields to what other motions? What other motions take precedence?	(k) Explained on pages
	PRIVILEGED MOTIONS									29–33
1	Fix time to which to adjourn	X^{r}	1	$\underline{N}$	Y	Y	$\underline{N}$	N	$\underline{N}$	32
2	Adjourn, unqualified	Z^{v}	2	N	N	$\underline{N}$	$\underline{N}$	$\frac{Y}{k}$	1	31
3	Take a recess	B_{r}	3	$\underline{N}$	Y_{q}	$\underline{N}$	$\underline{N}_{r}$	$\frac{Y}{k}$	1, 2	31
4	Raise question of privilege	F^{s}, w	4	N	N	N	N	/	1–3	30
5	Call for Orders of the Day	F_{s}, W	5	N	N	N	N	$\frac{Y}{C}$	1–4 VIII	29

[6]

SUBSIDIARY MOTIONS

										22–28
6	Lay on the table	O S, z	6	N	N	N	N	Ⓨ k	1–5; pending Incid.	27
7	Call for Previous Question	⅔	7	N	N	N	N		1–6; VIII Incid.	27
8	Limit, close, extend debate	⅔ g, n	8	N	Y	Y c	N		1–7 Incid.	26
9	Postpone to a certain time	G r	9	Y	Y m	Y	7, 8	Ⓨ k	1–8 Incid.	26
10	Commit or refer a main motion. Recommit	a	10	Y	Y	Y f	7, 8	Ⓨ k	1–9 Incid.	25
11	Amend an amendment		11	Y E	N	Y	7, 8	Ⓨ k	1–10; Incid. (exc. F, G)	24
12	Amend a motion	L	12	Y E	Y	Y	7, 8	Ⓝ	1–11; Incid. (exc. F)	23
13	Postpone indefinitely		13	Y R	N	Y Aff.	7, 8	Ⓝ	1–12 Incid.	23
14	MAIN MOTION		14	Y	Y	Y e	6–13	Y	1–13 Incid.	21
	MISCELLANEOUS MOTIONS— MAIN AND UNCLASSIFIED									40–46
I	Accept, adopt, approve a report		14	Y	Y	N Aff.	6–13		1–13 Incid.	43

[7]

(a)	(b)	(c)	(d)	(e)	(f)	(g)	(h)	(i)	(j)	(k)
Identification	RULES OF ORDER (For explanation of symbols, see pages 11–13.) See Note to Reader facing Chapter I for method of references to the Table in the text	Qualifications or restrictions	Rank or precedence	Is it debatable?	May it be amended?	May it be reconsidered?	Subsidiary motions applicable (besides Amend.)	May it be renewed?	Yields to what other motions? What other motions take precedence?	Explained on pages
	MISCELLANEOUS MOTIONS—*Cont.*									
II	Adopt constitution, bylaws, rules of order	⅔	14	Y	Y	N Aff.	6–13		1–13 Incid.	43
III	Amend constitution, bylaws, rules of order	⅔	14	Y	Y	N	6–13		1–13; Incid. (exc. E, F)	43
IV	Amend standing rules	⅔ p	14	Y	Y	Y	6–13		1–13 Incid.	45
V	Discharge a committee	⅔ y	14	Y	Y	Y	6–13		1–13 Incid.	46
VI	Committee of the Whole. Informal consideration of question	a	10	Y	N	N Aff.	6–13		1–9 Incid.	93
VII	Make a special order	⅔	14	Y	Y	N Aff.	6–13		1–13 Incid.	41

[8]

VIII	Reconsider	b, e,F	1st, i	u, D,R	N	N	N	6-9, K	d, k	N	40
IX	Rescind, repeal, annul	⅔ p	14	Y R	Y	N Aff	6-13		1-13 Incid.	45	
X	Take from the table	P x	MM	N	N	N	N	Y C	1-5 Incid.	41	
XI	Take up question out of order	⅔	14	N	N	N	N		1-4, 6 Incid.	41	
XII	Voting, motions relating to		14	N	Y	Y	6-13		1-13 Incid.	50-53	
	INCIDENTAL MOTIONS									34-39	
A	Appeal	F	CR	M	N	Y	6, 9	N	1-6 C	34	
B	Appeal on indecorum	F	CR	N	N	Y	6, 9		1-6 C	110	
C	Question of order	F s	BP	N	N	N	N	N	1-6	36	
D	Suspension of rules of order	⅔ h	BP QW	N	N	N	N	d	1-4, 6 Few Incid.	37	
E	Objection to consideration	F, ⅔ H, s	PQ	N	N	N Aff.	N	N	1-6	35	
F	Division of main question or amendment	t J	QW	N	Y	N	N		1-10	34	
G	Call for division of assembly in voting	F s	BP QW	N	N	N	N		N	50	

[9]

RULES OF ORDER

(For explanation of symbols, see pages 11–13.)

See Note to Reader facing Chapter I for method of references to the Table in the text

(a) Identification	(b)	(c) Qualifications or restrictions	(d) Rank or precedence	(e) Is it debatable?	(f) May it be amended?	(g) May it be reconsidered?	(h) Subsidiary motions applicable (besides Amend.)	(i) May it be renewed?	(j) Yields to what other motions? What other motions take precedence?	(k) Explained on pages
	INCIDENTAL MOTIONS—Cont.									
H	Permission to withdraw a motion	s	BP QW	N	N	N Aff.	N	╱	1–5	38
J	Create blank for purpose of amending		QW 12	Y	N	Y	7, 8	╱	1–11	25
K	Parliamentary inquiry or request for information	F s	BP QW	N	N	N	N	╱	1–5	37
L	Reading papers	s	BP	N	N	Y	N	╱	1–5	38
M	Prescribing method of nominations		BP	N	Y	N	N U	╱	1–5	54
N	Close nominations or polls / Reopen nominations or polls	⅔	BP	N	Y T	N	N	╱	1–5	54

EXPLANATION OF SYMBOLS

2/3   A two-thirds majority vote required to pass. Elsewhere only an ordinary majority vote is required.

1st   Gets *first* consideration; outranks all other motions.

a   Rules for motion "to commit" also apply to motion "to recommit," "to go into Committee of the whole," and "to consider informally." The last two, in the order given, rank next below the motion "to recommit."

A   After the vote has been taken under it.

Aff.   In the case of an affirmative vote.

b [11]   No question can twice be reconsidered unless it was materially amended after the first consideration.

B   To take a recess at a future time is a Main Motion.

BP   Outranks business pending.

c   Even though the order has been partly executed. Also, unless the motion "to close debate" and "to limit debate" have been reconsidered, the motion to which they are attached cannot be committed or postponed to a certain time.

C   After pending business is disposed of.

CR   First after Chair's ruling.

d   It cannot be renewed except by general consent.

D   Not when the motion to be reconsidered is undebatable.

e   Must be made by a person who voted on the prevailing side.

exc.   Except.

E   If the motion to which it refers is debatable.

f   Before the committee starts to act. But the committee can be discharged by a 2/3 vote. See Miscellaneous Motions, V.

F   May interrupt a speaker.

g   Motion "to limit debate" applies also to Subsidiary and Incidental motions and Reconsider if these are attached subsequently.

G   Not later than the next session. "Postpone to the next meeting" makes it a General Order. "Postpone to the next meeting and make a Special Order" requires a 2/3 vote. See note m.

h   Suspension of standing rules requires only a majority vote.

H   Applies only to Main Motions. See p. 21.

i   The making of the motion takes precedence over everything else, but its consideration may be deferred until the assembly has disposed of pending motions of higher rank than the one to be reconsidered.

Incid.   Incidental Motions.

J   May be applied even after the Previous Question has been ordered.

k   It cannot be renewed on the same day unless there is a sufficient change in affairs to make it a new question.

K   A motion "to reconsider," when immediately pending, may be laid on the table.

L   A motion "to amend" something already adopted is a Main Motion.

m   May be amended as to time (majority vote); or by making postponed question a Special Order (⅔ vote).

M   Not if it relates merely to indecorum or to transgression of the rules of speaking or to the priority of business; or if made during the division of the assembly or when the immediate pending question is undebatable. Otherwise it is debatable.

[12]

MM   Outranks Main Motions.

n   An order affecting limits of debate is in force only for the session in which it is adopted.

N   No, Not, or None.

N̲   No, Not, or None when privileged.

⊗   Not at the same session.

o   Out of order immediately after defeat of an "objection to consideration."

p   If no previous notice has been given. "To rescind" part of the constitution, bylaws, or rules of order previously adopted, both previous notice and a ⅔ majority are required.

P   May interrupt a speaker if his motion has not been stated by the Chair.

PQ   Outranks the pending question.

q   As to length.

QW   Outranks the question from which it arises.

r   The time for taking a recess or adjournment may be postponed by a ⅔ vote.

R   Opens the main question to debate, if the main question is or was debatable.

s   No second is required.

S   When the motion is habitually used to kill a question, a ⅔ vote is required.

t   A question cannot be divided unless it consists of distinctly independent propositions that can be separated.

T   As to time.

u   Undebatable if made after the Previous Question has been ordered. Then the main question also is undebatable.

U   When the election is pending.

v   Out of order when voting is in progress.

w   *Raising* a question of privilege should be distinguished from the privilege asked, which would require an ordinary Main Motion.

W   A call for Orders of the Day should be distinguished from the orders called for.

x   If the motion is passed, everything that was adhering to the question when it was tabled (except the motion "to postpone") is once more before the assembly. If a motion is taken from the table on the day after it was tabled, those who have exhausted the right to debate may speak again.

X   Privileged only (1) when another motion is pending and (2) in an assembly that has made no other provision for another meeting on the same or the next day.

y   Requires a ⅔ majority of all persons voting or an ordinary majority of the entire membership if no previous notice has been given.

Y   Yes.

Y̲   Yes, when progress in business warrants.

Ⓨ   Yes, when progress in discussion has changed the question materially.

z   If a motion is tabled, all adhering motions go with it.

Z   This motion loses its privileged character whenever it is qualified in any way and whenever its effect would be to dissolve the assembly permanently. It would then be debatable and amendable.

[13]

All references to "Table" in the text of this book are to the Table of Motions on pages 6 to 10. When the reference is to some specific motion, it is followed by the identification number or letter of that motion as printed in column (a) at the extreme left of the Table, and sometimes by a further column reference.

Thus, "(Table, 6)" refers the reader directly to the Subsidiary Motion "Lay on the table," identified as 6 in column (a) of the Table (in this case on page 7). "(Table, X, col. (d))" refers directly to the Miscellaneous Motion identified as X in column (a), with a further reference to column (d), "Rank or precedence."

By this means, all specific references to the Table of Motions are pinpointed, eliminating the need to search an entire page every time.

CHAPTER I

BUSINESS MEETINGS AND CONDUCT
OF BUSINESS

A. Kinds of Meetings

1. *Regular Meetings.* Those that are held at specified intervals, in accordance with the bylaws, to transact the regular business of an organization. A meeting may be interrupted by a recess; it is terminated by adjournment.

2. *Special Meetings.* Those that are called at particular times to deal with problems requiring special attention because of urgency or because more time is needed for their consideration than is available in a regular meeting. In a special meeting only that business may be discussed which was specified in the call for the meeting.

3. *Adjourned Meetings.* If a meeting—regular, special, or annual—is adjourned, i.e. closed to meet again on a certain later date (or even on the same day) specified in the motion to adjourn, the meeting, when it is resumed, is called an "adjourned meeting." It is a continuation of the preceding meeting and will deal with the business that was interrupted by adjournment. If there is a series of meetings for which the dates have been set, each meeting after the first is an "adjourned meeting," even though the motion to adjourn the previous meeting did not set a date for the next meeting. (Cf. Sessions, p. 16.)

4. *Annual Meetings.* In societies where offices are held for a calendar year, it is customary to hold an annual meeting for the purpose of
   a. Hearing reports of officers, boards, and committees for the year ended, and
   b. Electing officers, boards, and committees for the ensuing year.

An annual meeting may, in some societies, be the only meeting held during the year. In others it may be in addition to regular meetings held periodically throughout the year. It may be held on the same date as the last regular meeting and in connection with it. For the order of business in an annual meeting, see pp.99–100.

B. Sessions

A society may define "session" to suit its own purposes and adapt the rules of order accordingly. The following definition, however, is commonly accepted:

1. A session is a long meeting that, for the sake of convenience or because of necessity, is divided into shorter ones. A convention, even though it lasts for days, is regarded as a single session. Daily meetings of a session are terminated by adjournment, i.e. by bringing each daily meeting (except the last) to an end with the understanding that the transaction of business will be resumed on the following day or later on the same day. The continuity of business extends from the opening of a session to the close of it. This continuity may be interrupted but is not broken by adjournments or recesses.

2. Any meeting that is not an "adjourned" meeting (See "Adjourned Meetings" above) is regarded as belonging to a new session. Consequently a society's regular meetings, scheduled according to the Bylaws, are separate sessions. An "adjourned" meeting, however, would be a part of the same session as the last preceding regular meeting. A special meeting is a special session, i.e. one not on the regular schedule.

3. A session is closed *sine die,* "without day," i.e. no further meeting has been provided for, no provision has been made for reassembling. The usual motion for closing a session is "to adjourn *sine die.*" However, the use of the word "adjourn," which literally means "to a (specific) day" (*ad,* to, plus *jour,* day) cannot logically be used in connection with the phrase *sine die,* which means "without day." A more sensible formula for bringing a session to an end would be "that the meeting be closed *sine die.*"

4. A session must not extend beyond the date for electing new officers or at least not beyond the time when the new officers are inducted into office. Likewise it must not extend beyond the date of an annual meeting. Business may, of course, be postponed from one session to the next but not beyond that. Unfinished business is terminated with the end of a session. A motion made in a previous session cannot be reconsidered, but, if a society has sessions quarterly or more often, a motion "to reconsider" may be called up if it was made in the last previous session.

C. Quorum

No action taken in a business meeting of any organized society is legally binding unless a certain number of members was present. That number, usually specified in the Bylaws of the organization, is known as a *quorum*. It is the largest number of members that may reasonably be expected to attend meetings under ordinary conditions and a number that would be competent to transact business. Bylaws often specify a quorum of ⅓ or ¼ of the members. If a quorum is small and the business to be transacted is very important, it is wise to have more than a mere quorum present. The following rules concerning a quorum should be observed:

1. If the Bylaws do not specify a number, a quorum of an assembly is a majority of all the members.

2. A quorum of the delegates at a convention is a majority of those registered as present.

3. Sometimes a society is of such nature that it would be impossible to have a majority of members present at any time. If a business meeting of such an organization has been brought to the attention of all the members, then a quorum, unless the Bylaws provide otherwise, consists of the number of members actually present at the meeting.

4. In a committee meeting a quorum is a majority of the committee members, unless the society has ruled otherwise.

5. In a Committee of the Whole a quorum is the same as in a meeting of the assembly.

6. In meetings of Boards a quorum is determined by a vote of the assembly; if it has not been so determined, it is a majority of the members of the Board.

7. When there is not a quorum present, regular business cannot be transacted. Only the following steps are then in order:
   a. Make an effort to secure a quorum.
   b. Take a recess.
   c. Fix the time to which to adjourn.
   d. Adjourn.

8. If attendance falls below a quorum during the progress of a business meeting and if a member calls attention to the fact, the transaction of business is suspended pending a roll-call or counting of the members present. If the lack of a quorum is verified, all business and all discussion must come to an end, and the only steps that are in order are those listed above in ¶7.

D. Order of Business

A chairman, in conducting a business meeting, should follow the order of business laid down in the Bylaws of the society. The following order is typical:

1. Call to order.
2. Roll-call.[1]
3. Reading of minutes of the last previous meeting and their approval.
4. Reports of officers.
5. Reports of Boards.
6. Reports of standing committees.
7. Reports of special committees.
8. Unfinished business and general orders.
9. New business.
10. Adjournment.

Whether all of the reports listed above should be called for will depend on the kind of meeting. (See p. 15.)

E. Introducing Business

Whenever any business is brought to the attention of an assembly, the action to be taken on that business is proposed in the form of a "motion." [2] The member desiring to make a motion must get "the floor"; i.e., he must (1) *stand*, (2) *address* the chairman, and (3) *be recognized* by him. When he has made his motion, he should take his seat.[3]

Next, the motion must be seconded [4] by another member [5] and restated by the chairman. It is then ready to be discussed by the assembly, if it is a debatable motion; [6] e.g.—

MR. A (standing): Mr. Chairman (*or* Mr. President)[7]

---

1 If calling the roll requires too much time, as it may in a large assembly, some other device may be adopted for getting the attendance; e.g., members may be required to sign their names on rosters near the entrances or be checked by tellers posted at the doors.

2 Cf. p. 51.

3 If the assembly is a large one or if the speaker is not well known, he should give his name.

4 For the few motions that require no second, see Table.

5 The seconder need not rise or address the chair, unless the assembly is large, but he should give his name if the chairman does not know him. If there is no second, the motion is declared to be "lost for want of a second."

6 See Table, col. (e).

7 If the presiding officer is a woman, she is addressed as "Madam(e) Chairman" or "Madam(e) President" (N.B.: The word *madame* is French, denoting a married woman. However, the English form *madam* implies no such distinction.)

CHAIRMAN:	Mr. A.
MR. A:	I move that . . . (*or,* I move to . . .)
MR. B (seated):	I second the motion.
CHAIRMAN:	It has been moved by Mr. A and seconded by Mr. B that . . . (*he repeats the motion* [1]). Do you wish to discuss the motion?

Discussion follows. Each person desiring to speak must first get "the floor." Any person failing to observe this procedure is ruled "out of order."

A member is "out of order" if he rises while another still has the floor.

If two or more persons rise simultaneously and address the chairman, recognition will be given to—

1. One who has not previously spoken on the same question.
2. The one who made the motion.[2]
3. One who is opposed to the views of the last preceding speaker.

Any motion that is long or involved should be in writing and should be delivered to the secretary or clerk as soon as it is read.[3]

F. Discussion

In the discussion of a question observe the following points:

1. No member may speak more than twice on the same question during the meeting.
2. No member may speak a second time on the same question until others who have not spoken at all have been given an opportunity to speak.
3. No one may speak longer than ten minutes at one time, except by general consent or a ⅔ vote of the assembly.
4. Every speaker must confine his remarks to the question that is put before the assembly by the chairman. If he fails to do so, he is "out of order."
5. Members in a deliberative assembly are not permitted to address one another directly. All remarks must be directed to the chairman, who should be addressed as "Mr. Chairman," "Mr. President," or "Madame Chairman," "Madame President."
6. A speaker, when he refers to another member, should avoid using the person's name, if it is possible to do so. It is better to

---

[1] Especially if the motion was not distinctly heard by all.
[2] Or who introduced the series, if there is a series.
[3] For forms of resolutions, see pp. 131, 160.

say, "The member who . . . ," "The last speaker . . . ," etc.
An officer should be referred to by his title; e.g., "the Treasurer,"
"the Chair," "the Secretary," etc.

7. A member may not ask a question of a speaker without the consent of the chairman and then of the speaker. He should rise,
say "Mr. Chairman," and, having been recognized by him, say
"I should like to ask the speaker a question." The speaker must
stop immediately. The chairman then asks, "Will the speaker
answer a question?" If the speaker consents, the member asks his
question and gets his answer. However, the speaker is under no
obligation to answer a question, and, if he does not wish to
answer, the loss of time caused by the interruption should not be
counted against him.

8. Any member who, in speaking from the floor, refers to another
member in a discourteous or disrespectful manner or impugns
the motives of another or uses improper and offensive language
or is disorderly in any way, should be ruled "out of order." In
serious cases he may be required to apologize, and, if he refuses
to apologize, he may be disciplined by the assembly.

9. When a speaker is ruled out of order, he should take his seat
immediately. (See Appeals, pp. 34, 110, 132.)

10. A person who has made a motion is not permitted to speak
against it.[1]

11. A discussion may not be terminated by the chairman so long as
members still desire to speak on the question, except in accordance with rules mentioned above or in accordance with motions
that have been adopted to limit debate. (For these motions, see
p. 26.) If, however, the chairman gives adequate opportunity for
discussion and members do not respond and if he then puts the
question and the voting is begun, further attempts at discussion
will be "out of order."

12. The chairman should not permit the speaker to be disturbed by
heckling, whispering, walking across the room, or other annoy-
ances.

G. Putting the Question

The manner of putting the question and taking the vote is illustrated numerous times in the model proceedings of business meetings
on pp. 122–167.

---

[1] He may, of course, vote against it.

CHAPTER II

MAIN MOTIONS

A. Original Main Motions or Principal Questions

Motions that are aimed at getting some action on the primary items of business listed on the program of a business meeting are called Original Main Motions or Principal Questions. (See Table, 14.)

B. Incidental Main Motions

Some main motions are incidental to the transaction of business; e.g.—

Accept, approve, or adopt a resolution on a matter previously referred to a committee.

Amend a constitution or bylaws or rules of order or standing rules that have already been adopted.

Rescind or repeal.

Ratify.

Make a special order.

Take from the table.

Discharge a committee.

Motions relating to voting.

These are fully discussed on pp. 131–143. (See 1st Model Meeting—Main Motions, pp. 122–125. See also Table, I–V, VII, IX, XI, XII.)

Only one main motion can be immediately pending (i.e. "undecided," "awaiting decision," "undisposed of") at any one time. Any person who tries to make a main motion before a pending main motion is disposed of is "out of order."

CHAPTER III

SUBSIDIARY MOTIONS

Subsidiary motions are motions that apply to other motions. They have to do with procedure in handling the business presented at a meeting. (See Table, 6–13.) To a main motion (No. 14), any one of the subsidiary motions (No. 6–13) may be applied. Although only one main motion can be before an assembly at any given time, one or more or all of the subsidiary motions could be pending at the same time, each one to be disposed of in its proper order. Each of these, as you go up the scale on the Table, takes precedence over those below. A motion to

Postpone indefinitely (13) takes precedence over the original main question (14).

Amend the original question (12) takes precedence over *Postpone indefinitely* (13).

Amend an amendment (11) takes precedence over a motion to *Amend the original question* (12), *Postpone indefinitely* (13), and the original question (14).

Refer to a committee (10) takes precedence over No. 11–14.

Postpone to a definite time (9) takes precedence over No. 10–14.

Limit, close, or extend debate (8) takes precedence over No. 9–14.

Call for the previous question (7) takes precedence over No. 8–14.

Lay on the table (6) takes precedence over No. 7–14.

Every subsidiary motion takes precedence over every other subsidiary motion listed below it on the Table, and all subsidiary motions take precedence over the main motion or principal question. If all the subsidiary motions were made in the order just given (i.e. 13–6), they would all be "in order," they could all be attached to one main motion, and all could be pending at the same time. Each one in its turn would be "immediately" pending.

In voting, it would be necessary to dispose of No. 6 first, since it has the highest rank; then of No. 7, the next highest in rank; then of No. 8, and so on down the list. If motions No. 6, 9, 10, and 13 were lost, the vote would finally be taken on the main question.

Any subsidiary motion would be "out of order" if it were made while one of higher rank was pending; e.g., a motion to *Amend the main motion* would be "out of order" if a motion had been made to *Refer the original motion to a committee* and if this latter motion had not yet been disposed of. However, if a subsidiary motion of higher rank has been voted on and disposed of, one of lower rank would then be "in order."

The use of subsidiary motions is fully illustrated in the model procedure of Meeting No. 2, pp. 126–131, and of subsequent meetings. To find whether any given subsidiary motion is debatable or amendable, to what other motions it yields, and whether it may be reconsidered or have other subsidiary motions applied to it, consult the Table.

A. To Postpone Indefinitely

FORM: "I move to postpone action on the main motion indefinitely." This motion is self-explanatory. It has the lowest rank of all subsidiary motions. It is "out of order" if any one of the following motions is pending:

1. Another subsidiary motion (Table, 6–12),
   or
2. Any privileged question (Table, 1–5),
   or
3. Any incidental motion. (See pp. 34–39 and Table.)

If it has already been made and is pending, it yields to these. See illustration, p. 139. The purpose of this motion is to defeat a main question without risking a vote on it.

B. To Amend an Original Motion [1]

FORM: "I move to amend the motion by adding (or inserting) the word(s)[2] . . . .";

or

"I move to amend the motion by striking out [4] the word(s)[2] . . . .";

or

"I move to amend the motion by striking out [3] the word(s)[2] . . . . and adding (or inserting in its [their] place the word(s)[2] . . . ." [4]

---

[1] While the original motion is pending.

[2] The words must be consecutive.

[3] The words to be struck out should be voted on first, then those to be added or inserted.

[4] A motion to strike out something already adopted is a motion "to rescind" (See Table, IX. Also pp. 45, 165).

If an amendment involves a paragraph or an entire resolution, the following form is used:

> "I move to amend by substituting the following paragraph, viz., ..., for the paragraph .   .   .   .   .   ."; [1]
>
> *or*
>
> "I move to amend by substituting the following resolution for the pending resolution: viz., ..." [1]

A motion to amend the main motion takes precedence over the main motion and may be made at any time during the discussion of the main motion, provided that no motion of higher rank (e.g., No. 1–11; see Table) is pending.

During the discussion of the proposed amendment any debate of the original motion is "out of order." The proposed amendment must be disposed of before a vote can be taken on the original motion. If the amendment is carried, the main motion is then referred to as "the original main motion as amended." The Table shows which motions are amendable. (See illustrations in Model Business Meetings, pp. 122–167.) An amendment of a main motion is a primary amendment; only one amendment of this kind is in order at a time.

A proposed amendment is "out of order" if it—

1. Is irrelevant.
2. Reverses the Affirmative and Negative of the original question.
3. Repeats a question previously voted on in the same session.
4. Destroys the original question.
5. Changes the form of the motion to which it is applied.
6. Is absurd or frivolous.

A motion to amend a motion that has already been passed, or to amend the constitution, bylaws, standing rules, or rules of order, is not a subsidiary motion, but a main motion. (See Table, II–IV.)

C. To Amend an Amendment [2]

A primary amendment, discussed above, may be amended in the same manner as a main motion. Such an amendment, called a secondary amendment, however, cannot itself be amended. It takes precedence over the primary amendment and must be disposed of before the primary amendment can be put to a vote. If the secondary amendment is carried, the primary amendment is then referred to as "the amendment as amended." (Pp. 129–130.) An amendment to an

---

[1] A paragraph substituted for another can be amended only by *adding to it*.
[2] While the motion "to amend" is pending.

amendment must be relevant to both the primary amendment and the original motion. Only one amendment to an amendment is permissible at one time.

D. Filling Blanks

Sometimes in amending a motion there is a wide range of choice as to a specific number, date, amount, or name. In such cases the amendment is regarded (by general consent; see p. 51) as having a blank instead of a specific number, date, amount, or name. It would be best if the motion were made and seconded with the blank in it. It is then necessary to list all the suggestions [1] made for filling the blank and call for a vote on each, beginning with the largest number or the earliest date or the name first suggested. The voting is stopped as soon as one specific number, date, amount, or name has a majority of the votes. The figure or name that is thus chosen is inserted in the blank, and the motion is put to a vote.

The same procedure should be followed if several numbers, names, or dates are to be selected to fill a blank and if too many have not been proposed. If only as many are suggested as are required by the motion, they are inserted in the blank without a vote. (See p. 134.)

E. To Commit or Refer

FORM: "I move to refer the original question to a committee." [2]

"I move that the original question be referred to a committee of 5 (or 3 or 7) members appointed by the Chair."

"I move that the question be referred to the Committee on Membership (or some other standing committee)."

"I move that the Chair appoint a committee of 3 (or 5 or 7) members to study the question of . . . . and report suitable resolutions at our next regular meeting."

A motion to commit or refer is applied only to a main motion and may be made at any time during the discussion of (1) an original question, (2) a motion to postpone indefinitely, or (3) a motion to amend. If made while these are pending, it must be disposed of before

---

[1] These do not require motions; they are given informally when the chairman asks for them.

[2] If the mover does not specify which committee, in case it is a standing committee, or the size of the committee and how it is to be selected, in case it is a special committee, the chairman may ask the mover or the assembly for suggestions, which may be adopted by general consent or voted on in the order in which they are given. If committee members are to be elected, see rules on elections, pp. 56–71. If the number of members is left as a blank, see Amendment by Filling Blanks, above.

these can be voted on, since it outranks them. If it is carried, these
motions are dropped and never brought to a vote.

F. To Postpone to a Certain Time

FORM: "I move to postpone consideration of the question (or "that
the consideration of the question be postponed") to the next
meeting (or some other specific time)." [1]

Such a motion is in order at any time when any motion of lower
rank is pending (Table, 10–14) and when no motion of higher rank
is pending (Table, 1–8). For illustration of its use, see p. 127.

The motion is out of order if it—

1. Has the effect of postponing indefinitely or of defeating a
   motion.
2. Is applied to an entire class of business in advance; e.g., all
   reports of committees. [2]
3. Disregards the time set in the Bylaws. [3]

If a question is postponed to a certain time, it is treated as an
"order of the day" for that time and will precede New Business. (See
Orders of the Day, p. 29.)

The motion may also be made as follows:

"I move that the question be postponed until . . . . .
and that it be made a special order at that time." (See Special
Orders, p. 41.)

For the rank and qualifications of such a motion, see Table, VII.

G. To Limit, Close, or Extend Debate

FORM: "I move that debate on . . . . be limited
to . . . . . . minutes";
or
"I move that debate on . . . . be limited
to one 5-minute speech by each speaker."

FORM: "I move that the discussion period be extended . . . . .
minutes";
or
"I move that the discussion be extended to . . . . . .
o'clock."

---

[1] Not later than the next regular meeting.

[2] Any individual report may be postponed when it is called for.

[3] The Bylaws would not be violated by an "adjourned" meeting, i.e., a meeting that
was called in accordance with the Bylaws but could not be continued for some important reason, such as inadequate attendance, and therefore had to be adjourned to a
certain time.

FORM: "I move that the discussion be now closed";
> *or*

"I move that the discussion be closed at . . . o'clock."

When one of these motions is pending, another may be made as an amendment, provided that it does not conflict with the first; and, after one of them has been adopted, another may be made, if there is no conflict.

Any one of these motions may be made whenever there is discussion, if only motions of lower rank (Table, 9–14) are pending, and it must be disposed of before those of lower rank may be voted on. It is "out of order" if any motion of higher rank (Table, 1–7) is pending. For an illustration of its use, see p. 128.

NOTE: If one of these motions has been adopted but not reconsidered, the motions To Postpone to a Certain Time and To Commit can not be applied to the original question. (Table, 8, col. (g), note "c.")

H. Call for the "Previous Question"

FORM: "I call for the 'Previous Question' on the motion to . . .";
> *or*

"I call for the 'Previous Question' on the motion to . . . . . . and the amendment";
> *or*

"I call for the 'Previous Question' on the main motion and the motions adhering to it";
> *or*

"I call for the 'Previous Question' on all the pending motions."

This is a conventional and traditional way of saying "I move that the debate be stopped and that the question be put to a vote."

This motion is "in order" when any motion of lower rank (Table, 8–14) is pending. If made, it must be disposed of before those of lower rank may be voted on. It is "out of order" if a motion of higher rank (Table, 1–6, VIII, and Incidental Motions) is pending. For qualifications, see Table, col. (c); for an illustration of its use, see p. 130.

I. To Lay on the Table

FORM: "I move to lay the question on the table";
> *or*

"I move that the question of . . . . be laid on the table."

This motion can be applied only to questions actually pending; i.e., only to the one main motion under consideration at the time and to the subsidiary and incidental motions adhering to it. Its legitimate purpose [1] is to lay aside the pending questions temporarily until more urgent business has been attended to. It ranks above all other subsidiary motions (Table, 7–13) as well as above the main motion and must be disposed of before they can be voted on. It applies only to

1. Main motions, and

2. A motion To Reconsider.

If a main motion is "laid on the table," all motions adhering to it are likewise "tabled." While a motion is "on the table," no similar motion can be made. If a motion to "lay on the table" is lost, it may be renewed at any time after there has been substantial progress in debate or in the transaction of business. It is "out of order" if made immediately after the defeat of an Objection to Consideration (see p. 35; and Table, E).

A question "laid on the table" may remain there no longer than the end of the next session, if the organization has regular meetings quarterly or oftener. After that time the question is dead. (See motion To Take from the Table, p. 41; and Table, X.)

---

[1] It is often improperly used to suppress debate or kill a main motion.

CHAPTER IV

PRIVILEGED MOTIONS

A. Call for "Orders of the Day"

An organization usually has a definite order of business set forth in its Bylaws (see pp. 109–110), one of these being Special Orders (seė p. 41), i.e. questions assigned to certain hours. Other questions, to be discussed in a certain, specified order or on a certain day or at a certain meeting or in a certain session but not at certain, specified hours, are known as General Orders (see pp. 42, 147). Special Orders take precedence over General Orders. It is the duty of the chairman to see that these and all other orders of business are presented in their proper order and at the proper time, if a definite time has been set.

If the chairman, without authorization of the organization, should deviate from this order, any member has the right to demand that the proper order be adhered to. He should rise and, without waiting to be recognized, say "Mr. Chairman, I call for the Orders of the Day." [1] His call, if it is for Special Orders, may interrupt a speaker,[2] if necessary. The chairman must immediately interrupt whatever is being done and proceed to the special order of business that is due at the time. If it seems best to do so, he may put the question to a vote, thus: "Will the assembly now consider the Orders of the Day?" If ⅔ of those voting are opposed, the call is defeated (Table, D) and cannot be repeated until the pending business is disposed of.

When the hour arrives that has been assigned to a certain topic on a program, as in a convention, and there is a call for the Orders of the Day, the chairman should immediately put to a vote all pending questions and then announce the topic for that hour.

For qualifications and precedence of a call for the Orders of the Day, see Table, 5.

---

[1] The call must be general. A specific question cannot be demanded.

[2] If there are no Special Orders for that particular hour, the call for Orders of the Day must not interrupt pending business. It may, however, interrupt a speaker who is making or has made a main motion, provided that such motion has not been stated by the chairman.

B. To Raise a Question of Privilege

Questions of privilege are questions or motions relating to—

1. Privileges and rights of the assembly as a whole,[1] involved in conditions or circumstances or incidents that affect the dignity, honor, safety, welfare, or comfort of the group as a whole; e.g.[1]—
   a. Disorderly conduct of members, loud whispering, walking about, or other noises and disturbances.
   b. Disorder, misconduct, or confusion in the gallery.
   c. Misconduct or misrepresentation by news reporters and press photographers.
   d. Unsatisfactory conditions of the meeting place, such as poor ventilation or heating or lighting, inadequate equipment, or lack of other facilities for the comfort of members.

2. Privileges and rights of an individual member,[1] involved in—
   a. Charges against his character or conduct.
   b. Illness or inability to perform his duties.
   c. Requests to be excused from a meeting or from performance of a duty.
   d. Other personal requests that depend on the consent of the assembly or permission of the chairman.

FORM of the request or motion:

MR. A: Mr. Chairman, (*and then, without waiting to be recognized*) I rise to a question of privilege.[2]

CHAIRMAN: The member will please state his request.

MR. A: I move that the visitors be asked to leave the hall before the question is discussed.

The motion, having been made and seconded, is treated as an ordinary main motion and put to a vote. In some cases the chairman may grant the request without putting it to a vote; e.g.—

MR. A: Mr. Chairman, I rise to a question of privilege.

CHAIRMAN: The member will please state his request.

MR. A: I request that the speaker be asked to come to the platform to read his report.

---

[1] Questions in group No. 1 take precedence over those in group No. 2.
[2] This may not interrupt a speaker unless it is an urgent matter requiring immediate attention. Even though urgent, it is out of order while a vote is being taken.

CHAIRMAN: The request is granted. Will the speaker please come to the platform.

When a speaker raises a question that he calls a question of privilege, the chairman will decide whether it really is such and then will rule accordingly. Any two members, of course, may appeal from the chairman's ruling, forcing the matter to a vote. (See pp. 35, 132.)

Again, the chairman may rule that the question is a legitimate question of privilege but not important enough or urgent enough to justify interrupting the speaker. In such a case the speaker will resume and finish his speech, and the request for a privilege will be considered next. As soon as the question of privilege is disposed of, the business that was interrupted is resumed.

For qualifications and precedence of Questions of Privilege, see Table, 4.

N.B. See also Requests Incidental to the Transaction of Business, pp. 37, 38.

C. To Take a Recess

FORM: "I move to take a recess of . . . . minutes (or hours)";
or
"I move to take a recess until . . . . o'clock."

This motion is equivalent to a motion "to adjourn until a certain hour." Any intermission in the proceedings of one day is a recess, whether fixed by the hours of meeting, as provided for in the program, or ordered by a vote. After a recess the chairman calls the assembly to order and business is resumed at the point where it was interrupted by the intermission.

This motion is an unprivileged, main motion unless made while other business is pending.

For qualifications and precedence of a motion "to take a recess," see Table, 3; for an illustration of its use, see p. 130.

D. To Adjourn a Meeting

1. *To Adjourn* (unqualified).

FORM: "I move to adjourn."

The effect of this motion, when passed, is to bring a meeting to an end at once. It is not a privileged motion but a main motion if the time for the next meeting has not been set or if it would result in dissolving the assembly permanently. A motion "to adjourn," if qualified in any way, is a main motion.

A motion "to adjourn," when unqualified,

    a. Is "out of order"—
       1. If the time of adjournment has been set.[1]
       2. When another person has "the floor."
       3. While a vote is being taken or verified.
       4. If it is being used to obstruct the transaction of business.
       5. When it is unprivileged and another main motion is pending.
    b. Should not be permitted by the chairman—
       1. Until the time and place of the next meeting have been decided.
       2. If there are important announcements or other matters that must be brought to the attention of the assembly before adjournment.
    c. If defeated, may be renewed after progress has been made in the transaction of business.

After the motion has been made, no inquiry, appeal, or question of order should be permitted, except on matters requiring a decision before adjournment.

For the rank and precedence of this motion, see Table, 2. For examples of its use, see Model Business Meetings, pp. 122, 143, 150, 162, 167.

2. *To Adjourn "without day" (sine die).*

When a motion "to adjourn" closes not only the meeting but also the session, bringing all business to an end, a common form of the motion is: "I move to adjourn *sine die* (without day)." Such usage, however, is self-contradictory, violating the meaning of the word "adjourn." It would be more logical to say "I move that the assembly be dissolved." (See p. 16, Sessions, ¶ 3.)

3. *To Adjourn to a Specified Time.*

FORM: "I move that we adjourn to 8 P.M. tomorrow."

This motion, which serves the purpose of the two motions—"to adjourn" and "to fix the time to which to adjourn" (see ¶ E, following), is a main motion and is therefore out of order when any other motion is pending.

E. Fix the Time to Which to Adjourn

This motion is not a motion to adjourn; its purpose is to set the date for the next meeting. It outranks all other motions and is a

---

[1] A motion fixing the time of adjournment is a main motion. The time set for adjournment may be changed by a ⅔ vote. (See p. 46, ¶ L.)

privileged motion if made when another motion (e.g., "to adjourn") is pending.

Form of the motion, when privileged: "I move that, when we adjourn, we adjourn to 8 P.M. on next Monday." The place, if it has not already been decided, may be mentioned in the motion.

The motion may specify a time earlier (but not later) than the next regular meeting, if the time for the next regular meeting has already been set. This motion is a main motion—

a. If it is made when no other motion is pending.

b. If another meeting has already been set for the same day or the following day.

For qualifications and precedence of this motion, see the Table of Motions.

CHAPTER V

INCIDENTAL MOTIONS

A. Appeal

When a decision by the chairman seems to be in error, any member of the assembly may appeal from that decision. Immediately after the decision is announced, but not later, he should rise promptly and, without waiting to be recognized, even though another member has the floor, should say: "Mr. Chairman, I appeal from the decision of the Chair." The chairman then, having stated the issue involved, will put the question thus:

"Shall the decision of the Chair be sustained. Those in favor of supporting the decision will say 'aye,' " and, after taking the vote, "Those who are opposed will say 'no.' The decision is sustained (or reversed)."

For the rank and qualifications of an appeal, see Table, A. For illustration of its use, see p. 132.

The subsidiary motion "to lay on the table" may be applied to an appeal. If this motion is carried and if the main question adheres to the appeal (i.e., if the action on the main question is affected by the appeal), the main question also is laid on the table.

B. Division of a Question

The motion to divide a question into parts for convenience in discussion and in voting is applied only to main motions and amendments. It may be made even after the Previous Question (p. 27) has been ordered on the main motion.

When a main motion or an amendment has several parts and is capable of being divided into two or more independent propositions each of which could be acted on alone, it should be so divided, and each part should be considered and voted on separately. Division is usually done by general consent (p. 51) but it may be done by a formal motion.

FORM: "I move that the question be divided and considered in two (or more) parts, as follows: . . . . . (*specifying exactly how the division is to be made*)."

34

In the case of a complicated report or an elaborate and detailed proposition—such as bylaws, constitution, a series of resolutions, or a series of amendments—the form of the motion should be:

"I move to consider the . . . . . . by paragraph (section, article, resolution)";

or

"I move to consider the . . . . seriatim."

If a committee presents a series of separate and independent resolutions and moves the adoption of the entire series, a division must be made upon the demand of one person. A proposition that is single, however, no matter how complex it may be, cannot be divided, and in such a case a call for a division or a motion for division would be "out of order."

For precedence and qualifications of this motion, see the Table, F. For illustration of its use, see p. 136.

C. Objection to Consideration of a Question

When an original main motion or principal question (and no other) is irrelevant or contentious or unrelated to the objects of the society, the chairman may rule it "out of order." If he fails to do so, any member may, even when another has the floor, rise and object to the consideration, provided that the discussion has not yet started and provided that no subsidiary motion has yet been made.

FORM: "Mr. Chairman, I object to the consideration of the question."

The chairman must then put the question to a vote at once, thus:

"An objection has been raised to the consideration of the question. All those who are in favor of considering the question will say 'aye';" etc.

If a main motion has been rejected or postponed indefinitely and an attempt is later made to renew it (p. 48), the best way to defeat it is to object to the consideration of it.

An objection is "out of order" if applied to incidental motions that are necessary or relevant to the transaction of pending business or if applied to resolutions and reports presented at the request of the assembly. It may not, therefore, be applied to any of the following:

To adjourn, to rise and report, or to take a recess.

To set the time of adjournment.

To approve the minutes.

To set the time or name the place of the next meeting.

Nominations or the making of them.

For rank and qualifications of an Objection to Consideration, see Table, E. For an illustration of its use, see p. 131.

D. Question of Order

It is the duty of a chairman to see that the rules of order are observed. He shall not permit a motion that is contrary to the laws of the country or to the rules governing the organization or to fundamental principles of parliamentary procedure. If, however, a breach of the rules escapes the attention of the chairman or is disregarded by him, it is the privilege and the duty of any member who notices it to bring it to his attention and insist, if necessary, upon enforcement of the rule. In such a case the member will rise, address the chairman, even though someone else has the floor, and, without waiting to be recognized, state his purpose in rising, thus:

"Mr. Chairman, I rise to a point of order." The speaker, who has been interrupted, if there is one, will take his seat. The chairman will reply:

"The member may state the point."

The member then states what rule is being violated. If he is right, the chairman must correct the error at once. The speaker who was interrupted then has "the floor" once more.

If the question of order is such that the chairman cannot decide it or is in doubt as to the correct answer, he should ask the official parliamentarian, if there is one, or he may ask the advice of members whom he considers competent to decide the matter, or, if neither course is practicable, he may have the question decided by a vote of the assembly.[1]

If the question of order concerns indecorum (p. 20), the chairman decides whether there has been a breach of decorum or not. If his decision is in the negative, he permits the speaker to resume.[2] If he decides in the affirmative, he will not permit the speaker to continue, unless, an appeal having been made, he is ordered by the assembly to do so.

If the question of order relates to impropriety of language used in discussion, the chairman will caution the speaker about his language but will usually permit him to continue conditionally.

---

[1] Then the question is debatable if it does not relate to (a) precedence of motions, (b) the rules of debate (p. 19), or (c) indecorum; and if it was not raised while a vote was being taken.

[2] The time thus lost is not chargeable to the speaker.

E. Suspension of the Rules of Order

If an assembly finds it desirable or necessary to take some action that conflicts with the rules of order, it may, by a ⅔ vote, suspend temporarily the rule of order involved.[1, 2] A Standing Rule [3] may be suspended by an ordinary majority vote. Form of the motion:

"I move to suspend the rule that interferes with . . . . . ." [4]

This motion may be made even when another motion is pending, provided that it has a bearing on the pending question.[5]

For qualifications and precedence of the motion, see the Table, D. For an illustration of its use, see p. 154.

F. Requests Incidental to the Transaction of Business

1. *Parliamentary Inquiry*

If a member desires information on a parliamentary question, he should rise and, without waiting to be recognized, say:

"Mr. Chairman, I rise to a parliamentary inquiry."

The chairman will request him to state his inquiry and, if it is pertinent to the business pending, will answer it.

For qualifications and precedence of this motion, see Table, K, col. (d). For illustrations of its use, see pp. 132, 140.

2. *Request for Information*

If a member desires information other than parliamentary on the business pending, the procedure is similar to that in the case of a parliamentary inquiry—thus:

MEMBER (rising): Mr. Chairman, I rise for information.

CHAIRMAN: What is the member's question?

MEMBER: I should like to know . . . .

CHAIRMAN: (*Answers the question.*)

If the member wishes to ask the speaker a question:

MEMBER: Mr. Chairman, I should like to ask the gentleman a question.

CHAIRMAN: Is the speaker willing to answer a question?

SPEAKER: I am willing.

---

[1] No part of the constitution can be suspended.

[2] Rules of order included in the bylaws may be suspended temporarily. No other bylaws, however, may be suspended except according to provisions set forth in the Bylaws.

[3] See pp. 43, 111–113.

[4] The object of the suspension must be specific, and the suspension applies only to that object.

[5] A motion to suspend the rules cannot be made twice for the same purpose in any meeting, except by unanimous consent.

MEMBER: (*Addresses his question to the chairman.*)
SPEAKER: (*Answers the question, addressing the chair-
                   man.*)

The time consumed by question (or questions) and answer (or
answers) is taken out of the speaker's time. If, however, he is un-
willing to yield to a question, the time lost by the interruption is
not taken from his speaking time.

For qualifications and precedence of a request for information,
see Table, K. For an illustration of its use, see p. 132.

3. *Permission to Withdraw or Change a Motion.*

The author of a motion may, without asking the consent of anyone, withdraw or change his motion at any time before it is stated
by the chairman. After it has been stated by the chairman, however, it can be withdrawn or changed only by general consent (p.
51) or a vote of the assembly. When the request is made to withdraw or change a motion, the chairman will say:

"If there is no objection, the motion is withdrawn (or changed
as stated)."

If anyone objects, the chairman must put the request to a vote.

If a motion is withdrawn, any amendment or other motion adhering to it is also automatically withdrawn. A motion "to reconsider" can be withdrawn only by unanimous consent unless there
is still an opportunity to renew it.

If the author of a motion approves an amendment that has been
offered, he may accept the amendment and include it in his motion
by simply saying aloud, without obtaining the floor,

"Mr. Chairman, I accept the amendment."

If no objection is raised, the amendment is accepted, and the chairman announces the revised motion. If objection is made, the
amendment is treated in the usual manner (p. 50). If the author
of a motion alters his original motion in any way, the seconder is
at liberty to withdraw his second by simply announcing the fact.
It is then necessary to get a second for the revised motion. If there
is none, the revised motion is ignored by the chairman.

For qualifications and precedence of this request, see Table, H.
For an illustration of its use, see p. 133.

4. *Reading Papers to an Assembly.*

If papers or documents of any kind are presented to an assembly
for action, any member is entitled to have them read once before
a vote is taken, no matter how long they may be; he may even
demand that they be read again, if a second reading is necessary

to clarify a point in the debate or provide necessary information for an amendment. A request for permission to read papers for any other purpose, however—such as elaborating a speech or delaying the action on a pending question—is not granted except by general consent (p. 51), especially if the selections to be read are long. If an objection is raised, the request must be put to a vote.

Chapter VI

MISCELLANEOUS MOTIONS—MAIN
AND UNCLASSIFIED

A. To Reconsider a Vote

After a vote has been taken on a question, if a recount is desired, the following motion is used: "I move to reconsider the vote on the question of . . . ."
This motion—

1. Can be made only on the day on which the action was taken or on the next day of the session.
2. May be made only by a person who voted on the prevailing side.
3. May be made while another motion is pending [1] but not while a vote is being taken.
4. May interrupt a speaker, if necessary.
5. Is out of order if the desired result can be obtained in some other way or if the original motion may be renewed in a reasonable time.
6. If lost, cannot be renewed, except by general consent (p. 51).
7. Is debatable only when the motion to which it is applied is debatable.
8. May be "laid on the table" when immediately pending.
9. Takes precedence over everything else.

Although the making of this motion is highly privileged, its consideration has only the rank of the question that is to be reconsidered. Its consideration is in order as soon as the assembly has disposed of all pending motions of higher rank.

The motion *"to reconsider . . . . . . and have it entered on the minutes"* may be used to prevent the reconsideration from being called up until the next meeting. This form is sometimes used in large organizations that have small quorums and frequent meetings. It is an effective device for preventing a minority from imposing its will upon the majority.

---

[1] Even a motion to adjourn, if that motion has not yet been put to a vote.

B. To Take from the Table

    FORM: "I move to take from the table the question of . . . ."
This motion may be made at the same meeting at which the question
was tabled but not until there has been some progress in the transaction of other business [1]; or it may be made at the next meeting.[2]
It has the rank of a main motion and does not take precedence over
any other motion of any kind. However, a person rising to make such
a motion should be given preference over others who wish to make
other main motions.

    If subsidiary motions were adhering to a question when it was laid
on the table, they will still be adhering to it when it is taken from the
table [3] and must be disposed of in the order of their precedence or
rank.

    For qualifications of this motion, see Table, X. For an illustration
of its use, see p. 146.

C. To Take Up a Question Out of Proper Order

    This motion is a form of the motion "to suspend the rules" (see
p. 37).

    FORM: "I move to suspend the rules in order to consider
         . . . .";
        or
      "I move to suspend the rules that interfere with
         . . . .";
        or
      "I move to suspend the rules and adopt the resolution on
         . . . ."

A motion of this kind, to do something that is contrary to the established order of business, is often passed by general consent (p. 51);
i.e., the chairman asks whether there is any objection and, if there is
none, proceeds as if the motion had been passed. See Chap. V, Sect.
E and footnotes, p. 37. See also Table, XI.

D. To Make a Special Order

    1. *Of a question that is pending,* it is necessary to move
      "that the question be postponed to . . . .
      (a specific time) and that it be made a special order for that
      time."

---

[1] This rule applies also to the renewal of the motion "to take from the table" (See
Chap. VII).
[2] If meetings are held frequently (i.e., weekly, monthly, or quarterly).
[3] Except that, if the question is taken from the table at the next meeting after it was
tabled, the limitations upon debate, if any were voted, are no longer in effect.

See the subsidiary motion *To Postpone to a Certain Time,* p. 26.

For qualifications and rank of this motion, see Table, VII. For an illustration of its use, see p. 148.

2. *Of a question that is not pending:*

FORM: "I move that the question of . . . . be made a special order for . . . . (specifying a particular time)";

or the speaker may read a resolution (provided that such a matter is in order) and move

"that it be made a special order at the next (or some other) meeting (or at a particular hour)."

The same object may be accomplished by a motion to adopt a specified program or order of business. An assembly may, by a single vote, adopt a series of special orders, which would be the same as a program. The hour assigned to such topic must be strictly observed. If special orders are made at different times for the same meeting, they are brought up in the order in which they were made, regardless of the hours specified in the orders. When these orders are made, therefore, the chairman must not permit a subsequent order to have an earlier hour than a prior order; e.g., he must not permit a 7 P.M. order to be made after an 8 P.M. order has already been made.

If special orders are merely assigned to a certain meeting but to no particular hour, they will be brought under *Orders of the Day* (p. 29) if such a heading is provided in the order of business; if there is no such heading, they would come under *Unfinished Business.* When a question is made a special order for an entire meeting, it will be brought up immediately after the minutes of the last previous meeting have been read and disposed of.

All motions to make special orders are main motions. For qualifications and rank, see Table, VII.

E. To Make a General Order

A question that is postponed merely to a certain day is referred to as a General Order and is called up under *Orders of the Day* or immediately after *Unfinished Business* (see Order of Business, p. 17).

General Orders, if there are several questions postponed to the same meeting, will be considered in the order determined by their own respective ranks. If they are of the same rank, they will be dealt with in the order in which they were voted.

See *Postpone to a Certain Time,* p. 26; and *Orders of the Day,* p. 29.

F. To Accept, Adopt, or Approve a Report

FORM: 1. If the report is intended merely to inform the assembly:
"I move to accept the report of . . . . . ." [1]
2. If it recommends a course of action or offers resolutions: "I move to adopt (or approve) the report." [2]

If a financial report is made, it should be referred, without a motion or a vote, to the auditing committee.[3] If the auditing committee reports favorably, a motion is in order "to adopt the financial report."

A motion to accept or adopt or approve a report is a main motion. For its qualifications, see Table, I. For illustrations of its use, see pp. 123, 144–145.

G. To Adopt a Constitution, Bylaws, Rules of Order, or Standing Rules

Constitutions and bylaws are usually drafted by a committee especially appointed for the purpose, and the motion to adopt the constitution or bylaws thus drafted is the same as a motion to adopt the report of the committee. It is a main motion. For its rank and qualifications, see Table, II. For detailed procedure in considering constitutions or bylaws that are proposed for adoption, see pp. 143–145. For requirements of bylaws and for models, see pp. 106–111.

The Rules of Order used in ordinary societies and assemblies are rather uniform. Usually some standard manual is adopted as the authority. See pp. 111, 166.

Any organization may adopt special rules to fit its own needs, either in place of the standard rules of a manual or as a supplement to them. The rank and qualifications of a motion to adopt rules of order are the same as for adopting bylaws (see Table, II).

Standing Rules are administrative regulations that may be adopted without previous notice and by an ordinary majority from time to time as the need requires. The motion to adopt any standing rule is a main motion. For its rank and qualifications, see Table, II. For illustrations of standing rules, see pp. 111–113.

H. To Amend a Constitution, Bylaws, Rules of Order, or Standing Rules

FORM: "I move to amend the Constitution (or Bylaws, etc.),
Article . . . , Section . . . by . . . . . .
(See motion *To Amend*, p. 23.)

---

1 Such a motion should not be made by a member of the committee.
2 Such a motion may be made by the person reading the report.
3 If the bylaws do not provide for a standing auditing committee, the chairman should appoint a special committee, either as the result of a motion to that effect or by general consent (p. 51).

Although the language is the same as for an ordinary motion *To Amend,* this motion is not a subsidiary motion but a main motion,[1] and, like all other main motions, is subject to both primary and secondary amendments. (See Table, 11, 12; see also pp. 23, 24.)

For the rank and qualifications of this motion, see Table, III. For illustrations of its use, see pp. 143–145.

Constitutions and bylaws may be amended only in the manner prescribed in the constitution itself or in the Bylaws themselves; e.g.—

1. At any regular business meeting by a ⅔ majority of the members present and voting,[2] provided that the proposed amendment was submitted in writing [3] at the last previous business meeting; *or*

2. At any regular business meeting by a ⅔ majority of the members present and voting, provided that notice was given [4] at the last previous regular business meeting.

In all cases previous notice should be required, and the vote should be a ⅔ majority, even in cases where no rules to that effect have been adopted. However, if no rules have been established, amendments may be adopted at any regular meeting by an ordinary majority of the entire membership where such procedure is practicable.

If an organization holds only one regular meeting each year, obviously the only kind of previous notice that is practicable is a notice sent by mail to all members.

If an assembly authorizes the appointment of a committee to revise the Constitution or Bylaws and report at a certain meeting, such action is regarded as sufficient previous notice, if there is no stipulation to the contrary. All members should be notified of the date on which the revision is to be voted upon.

Amendments to a Constitution, Bylaws, or rules of order become effective immediately after their adoption unless some later time was previously agreed upon or specified in the motion "to revise" or the motion "to adopt the revision."

When proposed amendments to the Constitution, Bylaws, or rules of order are being discussed by the assembly on the date announced, motions to amend these are in order and are, of course, subsidiary motions (pp. 23, 24) requiring only an ordinary majority and no previous notice. However, if a subsidiary motion "to amend the pend-

---

1 See footnote 4 on page 23.

2 Provided a *quorum* is present.

3 Unless specified to the contrary, the exact wording of the proposed amendment need not be given in the notice.

4 The previous notice may be oral if there is no provision to the contrary.

ing amendment" is not strictly relevant to the change under discussion but proposes a change other than the one referred to in the previous notice or a change greater than the one mentioned, it is "out of order," for then it is a main motion in substance and requires previous notice.

Standing rules may be amended at any regular meeting by a ⅔ vote without previous notice or by an ordinary majority if notice was given. The vote may also be reconsidered. See Table, IV.

I. To Rescind, Repeal, or Annul

FORM: "I move to rescind the vote on the question of . . . .";
> *or*

"I move to rescind the action taken on the question of . . . ."

The motion "to rescind" has the effect of destroying or canceling something already adopted. It is a main motion and may be applied only to an action or vote already taken on a *main* question. It is "out of order"—

1. If a motion "to reconsider" the same question has been made but has not yet been acted upon; [1]

2. If it ("to rescind") comes too late to prevent carrying out the action that was authorized;

3. If the result would be the violation of a contract; or

4. If it applies to the acceptance of a resignation or to a notice of expulsion when the member who is resigning or being expelled has already been notified.

The motion "to rescind" may contain the additional words "and expunge from the record." A majority vote of the entire membership should be required to pass the motion in this form.

When a motion "to rescind" has been carried, the secretary should make a notation to that effect on the margin of the record opposite the matter rescinded. If it was voted also "to expunge it from the record," he should strike out the words indicated and sign his name and the date of the action.

The word *rescind,* meaning "destroy," is the term most commonly used in this motion, although *annul* ("nullify," "cancel," "invalidate") and *repeal* ("recall," "revoke") are sometimes used. There is no practical distinction.

For the rank and qualifications of this motion, see Table, IX.

---

[1] Because a motion "to reconsider" takes precedence over a main motion.

J. To Discharge a Committee

A special committee automatically ceases to exist as soon as it has done its work and made a report that was accepted. In such cases a motion "to discharge" is not necessary. If, however, a committee has not yet finished its assignment or made a report that was accepted and if it is too late "to reconsider" [1] the vote that referred the matter to the committee, the assembly may, if it wishes, take the question out of the hands of the committee. The form of the motion necessary for this purpose is as follows:

"I move that the committee be discharged from further consideration of . . . ."

If previous notice has been given, a majority vote is sufficient for passage; if not, a ⅔ vote of those present and voting or a majority vote of the entire membership is required. If this motion is carried, the question that had been referred to a committee may, by means of a motion and a vote, be brought up for discussion by the assembly as a whole.

K. To Ratify or to Censure

When it is doubtful whether an action taken by an officer or other representative of an assembly was within his authority, a motion "to ratify" may be offered to test the matter.

FORM: "I move to ratify the action taken by . . . . . ."

When it is desired to show disapproval of an action, a motion "to censure" is appropriate.

FORM: "I move to censure . . . . . for . . . . ."

Either motion is a main motion, requiring only a majority of votes for passage. Either motion may be amended by substituting the other.

L. To Extend the Time Previously Set for Adjournment or Recess

When the time set for adjournment [2] or recess has arrived, it may be postponed by a ⅔ vote. This motion is not debatable.

FORM: "I move to extend the time of adjournment (or recess) to . . . ."

M. Motions Pertaining to Nominations, see p. 54

N. Motions Pertaining to Voting, see pp. 50–52

---

[1] Reconsideration must be done on the day on which the motion "to commit" was passed or on the following day (See p. 45, note 1). Even then the motion "to reconsider" is "out of order" if the committee has already taken up the discussion of the question (See Table, VIII, col. (g).)
[2] See p. 32, note.

Chapter VII

DILATORY, ABSURD, OR FRIVOLOUS MOTIONS

Motions that are absurd or frivolous or that are obviously intended merely to obstruct the transaction of business are prohibited, no matter in what parliamentary form they are expressed. Among those commonly so abused are the following:

To Adjourn, To Take a Recess (pp. 31–33).

To Amend (pp. 23, 24).

Appeal (p. 34).

Question of Order (p. 36).

Division of the Assembly (p. 50).

To Lay on the Table (p. 27).

To Postpone (pp. 23, 26).

To Reconsider (p. 40).

Renewal of a Motion (pp. 48, 49).

All these motions have a legitimate use and when so used are "in order," but, if they are absurd, are used insincerely or for the sake of comedy or as dilatory tactics, the chairman should rule them "out of order." Persons employing such obstructive tactics should be warned by the chairman, and, if they persist in disregarding the warning, they should, at the direction of the chairman, be ejected from the meeting by the sergeant-at-arms (p. 117, ¶ 9).

Chapter VIII

RENEWAL OF MOTIONS

Certain motions, if defeated, may be renewed under certain conditions. In general, they cannot be renewed under circumstances or at times which permit them to be "taken from the table" or "reconsidered" or at a meeting at which they were postponed. The rules are as follows:

PRIVILEGED MOTIONS	*May the motion be RENEWED?*
1. Fix Time to Which to Adjourn.	No.
2. Adjourn (unqualified). 3. Take a recess.	Yes, when progress in business warrants.
5. Call for Orders of the Day.	Yes, after pending business is disposed of.

SUBSIDIARY MOTIONS	
6. Lay on the Table.	Yes
9. Postpone to a Certain Time.	Yes — When progress in discussion has
10. Commit or Refer.	Yes — changed the question materially.
11. Amend an Amendment.	Yes
12. Amend a Motion. 13. Postpone (main motion) indefinitely.	No, not at the same session, unless the motion was previously withdrawn.

14. MAIN MOTIONS

Yes: (a) At the next session, if
- (1) Meetings are frequent (quarterly, monthly, weekly, etc.).
- (2) Motion was not postponed to that session.
- (3) Motion is not "reconsidered" at that session.
- (4) Motion was not "laid on the table" at preceding session.
- (5) Motion was not "postponed indefinitely."

    (b) Otherwise at the following session.

MISCELLANEOUS MOTIONS—MAIN AND UNCLASSIFIED

VIII. Reconsider.	No, unless in the previous consideration the question was materially changed by amendment.
X. Take from the Table.	Yes, after pending business is disposed of.

INCIDENTAL MOTIONS

A. Appeal.	No, if the appeal is the same as it was before.
C. Question of Order.	No, if the same point was previously made and lost in the same session.
D. Suspend the Rules.	No, not at the same meeting and for the same purpose, but permissible in later meeting, even on the same day.
E. Objection to Consideration.	No.
12. Correct the Minutes.	Yes, if there is justification.

NOTE: *The motions are identified as in the Table, Col. (a).*

CHAPTER IX

MOTIONS AND REGULATIONS PERTAINING TO VOTING

A. Call for a Division of the Assembly

The chairman, when he puts a question, may, if he has a choice, require any one of three types of vote—a voice vote, a vote by a show of hands, or a standing vote. He should, however, use good judgment. If there is a prospect that the vote will be close, he should require, not a voice vote, in which there might be some doubt or dispute about the decision, but a standing vote, where the outcome can be determined without question.

If a vote is taken by voice or by a show of hands and there is a reasonable doubt about the outcome, any member of the assembly may, without rising or addressing the chairman, demand a division of the assembly, or standing vote. He needs merely to call out "Division" or "I call for a division." The chairman must then immediately put the question again, this time requiring a standing or rising vote. The call for a division may be made as soon as the question has been put or after the vote has been taken and the outcome announced. It may even interrupt a speaker, but it must be made before another motion is presented.

For qualifications and precedence of Division of the Assembly, see Table, G. For an illustration of its use, see p. 135.

B. Tie Vote and the Chairman's Vote

If a vote is a tie, the motion being voted on is lost. When only one vote is lacking to make a tie, the chairman, if he is a member of the assembly and if he has not already voted, may exercise his right to vote and declare the vote a tie. If the tie vote is on an appeal from the decision of the chairman, the appeal is lost, even though the tie resulted from the chairman's vote.

If a vote is a tie, the chairman has the right to break the tie by his own vote, but he is not compelled to do so. In some instances he may find it diplomatic to waive his right to vote. If a motion requires a ⅔ vote to pass and one vote is needed to make the ⅔, the chairman may vote with the majority if he wishes to. If he declines to vote, the motion is lost.

If voting is by ballot, the chairman, like any other member of the assembly, has the right to vote, regardless of the outcome.

C. Change of Vote

After a member has voted, he may change his vote at any time before the result has been announced by the chairman, unless the voting was done by ballot. The chairman, however, should be alert against fraud in such a change.

D. Voting by General (or Unanimous) Consent

Routine matters, business of minor importance, non-contentious proposals, and other matters where there is no minority to protect may often be disposed of by silent assent and without the formality of a motion or vote. In such cases the chairman merely needs to say:

"If there is no objection, the proposal is adopted." (cf. p. 41)

If, however, an objection is raised, the chairman must require a regular vote. The reading of the Minutes of the Last Previous Meeting is an instance of routine business that is usually disposed of by General Consent. After the minutes have been read, corrections may be made and adopted without a motion or a vote. When all needed corrections have been made, the chairman says:

"If there are no further corrections, the minutes stand approved as read and corrected."

In most business meetings there are many matters that could be handled expeditiously and economically by the informal procedure of General Consent. However, this procedure cannot be used and should not be attempted in the following cases:

1. When the question may possibly be controversial.

2. In any matter where there might be a minority opinion.

3. In any matter affecting the rights of absent members.

4. In any case where a secret ballot is required by the Bylaws or by the standard rules of procedure.

E. Roll-call for Voting

When it is desired to keep a record of the vote of each member upon a specific question that is to be decided in the affirmative or the negative, an assembly may, by a majority decision, order a vote to be taken by roll-call.

FORM: "I move to count the vote on this question"; *or* "I move that the vote be taken by roll-call"; *or* "I move that the vote be taken by 'yeas' and 'nays.'"

This motion is undebatable. (See Table, XII.) If it is passed, each member, as his name is read by the secretary, will answer "aye" or "no." If a member is present but does not wish to vote, he may merely answer "present."

MODEL FORM

Members		"Aye"	"No"	"Present"	Absent
Mr. A		1			
Mr. B			1		
Mr. C			1		
Mr. D		1			
Mr. E		1			
Mr. F				1	
Mr. G			1		
Mr. H		1			
Mr. I					1
	Total	4	3	1	1

When the roll-call is completed, the secretary, in order to avoid errors, should read aloud the names of those who voted "aye," then the names of those voting "no," and finally the names of those who merely said "present." He should then read the total number of those voting *for* and the total number of those voting *against* the motion. The chairman will announce the result of the vote. The secretary will preserve the roll-call record and make it a part of the Minutes. He should have a supply of the model forms shown above to be used as occasions require.

F. Voting by Ballot in General Matters

In the election of officers, the reception of new members, and the trial of an officer or member it is customary, though not necessary, to vote by ballot. The Bylaws of an organization usually require a ballot vote in such instances and may specify it in others. Even in cases where ballot voting is not specifically required it is permissible and may be ordered by a majority vote. (The motion is undebatable. See Table, XII.) It is generally desirable where many of the members do not want their attitudes made public.

When the Bylaws of an organization require a vote by ballot, any other kind of vote is unconstitutional, and a motion proposing to substitute any other kind of voting is "out of order." If the law guarantees the right to vote by ballot on a specific question, the substitution of any other type of voting is illegal.

When a vote by ballot is not unanimous, any motion "to make it unanimous" or "to instruct the secretary to cast a (unanimous) ballot" is "out of order," since it would conflict with the purpose of the motion or Bylaw requiring a ballot vote and would make it necessary for a minority member, despite the previous assurance of secrecy, to reveal his vote and, if it caused him to remain silent, would amount to depriving him of his constitutional privilege.

If the vote to be taken by ballot merely requires the voter to say "yes" or "no," the secretary should provide slips of paper of uniform size and kind, which will be delivered to tellers appointed by the chairman and distributed by these to all persons eligible to vote, including the chairman. When these have been distributed, the chairman will inquire whether anyone has been overlooked.

After all members have received ballots and have had time to mark them with the word "yes" or the word "no," at a signal from the chairman the tellers will collect the ballots and verify the count, checking the number of ballots against the number of voters. At the request of the presiding officer, the chairman of the tellers will read the totals, which he has recorded in the model form below. He will then deliver this report to the secretary.

Result of the Balloting on the Question of
. . . .

Number of ballots cast	80
Majority needed to pass	41
Number in favor of the proposition 50	
Number opposed to the proposition 28	
Illegal ballots 2	

TELLERS: R. W. Arthur, CHAIRMAN
H. C. Knowles
J. D. Ross

CHAPTER X

NOMINATION OF OFFICERS

A. Motions Pertaining to Nominations

The method of making nominations for any office is usually prescribed in the Bylaws or the rules. Where the method is not so designated, any member of the assembly may make a motion to decide the procedure. Such a motion is *incidental* if made while the election is pending. (See Table, M.) At any other time it is a main motion. In any case it is undebatable.

A motion may specify nominations by any of the following methods:

1. By the chairman.
2. From the floor; i.e., by the members.
3. By a committee.
4. By ballot.
5. By mail.

FORM: "I move that nominations for the office of . . . . . . be made . . . . . ."

B. Nominations from the Floor

If nominations are made from the floor, i.e. by the members, the procedure is as follows:

1. The chairman declares nominations "in order" for a specific office.
2. A member rises, is recognized, and says, "I nominate Mr. . . . . . for the office of . . . . . ." A nomination does not need to be seconded.
3. The chairman announces that "Mr. . . . . . has been nominated," and the clerk enters the nominee's name on the slate of candidates.
4. Other nominations are made in the same manner. No person may nominate more than one candidate for an office.
5. When no further nominees for an office are presented, the chairman declares the nominations closed for that office. At any time

after a reasonable number of candidates has been nominated, any member may move "that the nominations be closed," but this motion is "out of order" if it interrupts nominations that are in progress or if the slate of candidates, as required by the Bylaws, is incomplete. A ⅔ vote is necessary to close nominations.[1] (See Table, M.)

6. The same procedure is followed for each succeeding office.

C. Nominations by Committee

If nominations have been made by a committee, the chairman will ask whether the assembly wishes to name other candidates. Candidates nominated from the floor, if there were any, would be added to those recommended by the committee. (See p. 155.)

---

[1] If, after nominations have been closed, it seems necessary to reopen them, a motion "to reopen nominations" may be passed by a majority vote. (See Table, N.)

CHAPTER XI

ELECTION OF OFFICERS

A. General Procedure

Election procedure, in its simplest form, is as follows:

1. When the slate of candidates is complete for an office, the chairman instructs the clerk to supply blank ballots (which usually have been prepared for the occasion) and appoints tellers to distribute these to the voters.

2. When sufficient time has been allowed for marking the ballots, the chairman orders the tellers to collect and tally the ballots.

3. When the ballots have been counted, the chairman of the tellers (i.e. the first one named, unless specified otherwise) addresses the presiding officer, is recognized, and reports as follows:

"Mr. Chairman, the result of the balloting for the office of

. . . . is as follows:

Number of ballots cast 80
Number necessary for election 41
Mr. G received 42
Mr. H received 21
Mr. M received 17

TELLERS: J. C. Roberts, CHAIRMAN
R. W. Forman
D. L. Kennedy"

4. The chairman announces the outcome of the vote; e.g., as in the illustration, "Mr. G, having received a majority of the votes cast, is elected to the office of . . . ."

5. The other offices are dealt with in the same manner, one at a time. If, in the case of any office, no candidate receives a majority of the votes cast, the balloting will have to be repeated (see p. 60, note; p. 61, ¶ 3.)

6. When the election is completed, the chairman declares the election ended, and the tellers' report with the tellers' signatures, as shown above, is delivered to the secretary for recording in the Minutes.

In small organizations, where little time is required for balloting and counting the votes, the simple procedure outlined above is satisfactory and customary. In many situations, however, it might be unsatisfactory for electing officers; e.g.—

1. If an organization is very large and there are many ballots to be counted.

2. If there are many offices to be filled, even though the organization is not very large.

3. If there is little prospect of electing on the first ballot.

4. If there is no time or if the time is insufficient for taking a second and a third ballot and reporting the results.

In such cases it would be better to use the Preferential Ballot, explained and illustrated on pp. 61–63, under Absentee Balloting by Mail.

B. Electing Members of Boards and Committees

Where several members are to be elected to a board or council or committee, each voter, of course, will mark the required number of names on his ballot. If, for instance, five members are to be elected out of thirteen candidates, an individual ballot might appear as on p. 58.

If printed or mimeographed ballots were not used, each voter would write out on plain paper the names of the five candidates of his choice. These could be arranged in any order and the tabulation of votes on the first ballot might appear as in the example on p. 59.

	BALLOT FOR BOARD OF DIRECTORS VOTE FOR FIVE (5)
	Mr. Randolph
X	Mr. Brown
	Mr. Winston
	Mr. Darrow
X	Mr. Stevens
X	Mr. Allen
X	Mr. Prentiss
	Mr. Goodman
	Mr. Carter
	Mr. Lawrence
X	Mr. Miller
	Mr. Knight
	Mr. Freeman

TABULATION OF VOTES			
Number of persons voting . . . . 50 Number of votes on each ballot . . . . 5 Number of votes necessary to elect 26			
For Directors	*Tally*	*Total votes*	*Majority received*
MR. RANDOLPH	///// ///// /////	15	
MR. BROWN	///// ///// ///// /////	20	
MR. WINSTON	///// ///// //	12	
MR. DARROW	///// ///// ///// ///// ///// ///// ///// ///// ///// /////	50	Elected
MR. STEVENS	///// /////	10	
MR. ALLEN	///// ///// /////	15	
MR. PRENTISS	///// ///// ///// ///// //	22	
MR. GOODMAN	///// ///// ///// /	16	
MR. CARTER	///// ///// ///// ///// ///// ///// ///// /////	40	Elected
MR. LAWRENCE	///// ///// ///// ///// ///// ///// //	32	Elected
MR. MILLER	//	2	
MR. KNIGHT	///// /	6	
MR. FREEMAN	///// /////	10	
	Total	250	

If fewer than the required number received a majority of the votes on the first ballot, as in the illustration above, it would be necessary to take a second ballot on the *remaining* names.[1] The tabulation of the votes on the second ballot might appear thus:

Number of persons voting . . . . 50 Number of votes on each ballot . . . . 5 Number of votes necessary to elect 26			
For Directors	*Tally*	*Total votes*	*Majority received*
MR. RANDOLPH	ⱈⱈⱈ ⱈⱈⱈ ⱈⱈⱈ ///	18	
MR. BROWN	ⱈⱈⱈ ⱈⱈⱈ ⱈⱈⱈ ⱈⱈⱈ ⱈⱈⱈ //	27	Elected
MR. WINSTON	///	3	
MR. STEVENS		0	
MR. ALLEN	////	4	
MR. PRENTISS	ⱈⱈⱈ ⱈⱈⱈ ⱈⱈⱈ ⱈⱈⱈ ⱈⱈⱈ ////	29	Elected
MR. GOODMAN	ⱈⱈⱈ ⱈⱈⱈ ⱈⱈⱈ //	17	
MR. MILLER		0	
MR. KNIGHT		0	
MR. FREEMAN		2	
	Total	100	

[1] Before the second ballot is taken, a motion would be "in order" to strike from the list the names of those who received only a few votes on the first ballot. A majority vote would be necessary to authorize such action.

In the illustrations given above the tabulations show that three directors were elected on the first ballot and two on the second. If only one had been elected on the second ballot, it would have been necessary to take a third ballot. If on the second ballot the two highest candidates received an equal number of votes, both candidates would be declared elected.

If on the first ballot one more than the required number of persons received a majority of the votes cast, it would be necessary to reballot on the *two lowest,* or possibly the *three lowest* if the margin of difference were small.

If on the first ballot *no* candidate received a majority of the votes, it would be necessary to strike out [1] the names of the lowest and take a second ballot.

In the election of members of a committee sometimes those receiving the most votes—regardless of whether the number is a majority or not—are declared elected. This procedure—electing by a *plurality* vote—is unparliamentary unless it is specifically provided for in the Bylaws or authorized by a majority of the society. Even then it is often a source of dissatisfaction, especially when the votes of the winners do not far exceed the votes of the losers, and when the winners do not all have majorities.

C. Absentee Balloting by Mail

In many organizations where members are widely scattered and cannot all be present to vote in person, the Bylaws may provide that the election of officers, amendments to the Constitution or Bylaws, and perhaps certain other matters may be voted upon by mail. In such cases the ballots sent to the members should be uniform and printed or mimeographed, as in the illustration on p. 62.

It will be noted that in such cases the ballot is not strictly secret, for the voter must sign his name. Consequently how he voted would be known to the tellers, at least, and possibly to the Secretary. In routine matters, of course, which are commonly decided in a meeting by a voice vote or by a division, a member could have no objection to sending a signed ballot by mail. However, in matters where secrecy is important or desirable and where a secret ballot is guaranteed by the Bylaws, voting should not be done by mail.

---

[1] A motion carried by a majority vote would be necessary to authorize such procedure. See footnote on p. 60. See also p. 159.

```
┌─────────────────────────────────────────────────────────────┐
│ YES                     Question to be voted on:              │
│  ┌──┐   Should the Bylaws of the  . . . . . . .  Club,        │
│  │  │   Article  . . . .  Section  . . . .  be amended to     │
│  └──┘   read as follows:                                      │
│  ───       " . . . . . . . . . . . . . . . . . .              │
│ NO         . . . . . . . . . . . . . . . . . . .              │
│  ┌──┐      . . . . . . . . . . . . . . . . . . .              │
│  │  │      . . . . . . . . . . . . . . . . ."?                │
│  └──┘                                                         │
├─────────────────────────────────────────────────────────────┤
│ Note 1.  Put a cross in one of the boxes to the left of the   │
│          question above.                                      │
│ Note 2.  Seal this ballot in the enclosed envelope marked     │
│          "Tellers," and                                       │
│ Note 3.  Mail in a larger envelope to—                        │
│            . . . . . . . . . . . . . . . . . .                │
│            . . . . . . . . . . . . . . . . . .                │
│            . . . . . . . . . . . . . . . . . .                │
│                                                               │
│ Signature of voter _____    │
│          Address _____    │
│                  _____    │
│                                                               │
└─────────────────────────────────────────────────────────────┘
```

Any necessary explanation of the meaning of the proposition to be voted on or the arguments for and against it may, if it seems desirable, be printed or mimeographed on a separate sheet and sent out with the ballots.

Absentee ballots for an election of officers may not differ from the printed or mimeographed ballots ordinarily used in an election meeting, except for the directions for mailing and the space for the signature. However, since the outcome of the balloting might be that no nominee received a majority of the votes cast, and therefore no one was elected, and since it would be cumbersome and impractical to take a second ballot, it is wise to use a *preferential ballot* or single transferable vote.

D. Preferential Ballot—Single Transferable Vote

On a ballot of this kind a voter is required to rank all candidates, listing his 1st, 2nd, 3rd, 4th choice, etc., as follows:

BALLOT FOR PRESIDENT

Nominees	Order of Preference
MR. G	2
MR. R	1
MR. B	3
MR. H	4

The voter may, of course, reject one or more of the nominees on the ticket and write in other choices on the blank lines at the bottom of the ballot. Instructions to this effect should be printed on the ballot.

The tellers, when they count the votes, will stack the ballots in piles, one pile for each candidate who is marked *1st choice*. The ballots in each pile are then counted thus:

	1st Choice
MR. G	20
MR. R	17
MR. B	11
MR. H	9
Total votes	57
Needed to elect . . .	29

If a candidate has received a majority of *1st choice* votes, he is elected. If, however, no candidate has a majority of *1st choice* votes, as in the illustration above, the name of the nominee who polled the smallest number of *1st choice* votes is struck from the list, and the votes that he received are transferred to the candidates marked *2nd choice* on his ballots. If now any candidate has a majority of votes, he is elected. If, however, no candidate as yet has a majority, the lowest candidate is dropped, and his votes are transferred to the candidates marked *3rd choice* on the ballots that he received, and so on until one candidate has received a majority and is elected.

In case the winner must be one of the last two surviving candidates and these two are tied, the one who polled the greater number of *1st choice* votes should be declared the winner. If both had received the same number of *1st choice* votes, however, the candidate with the larger number of *2nd choice* votes would be the winner. If there were a tie in the *2nd choice* votes, the nominee with the greater number of *3rd choice* votes would be declared elected. If there should be a tie here too, it would be necessary to draw lots or use whatever other method might be specified in the Bylaws.

Following is an illustration of the method of tabulating preferential votes:

Nominees	Column I	Column II		Column III		
	First Choice	Transf. of Mr. H's Vote	Result	Transf. of Mr. B's Vote	Result	
MR. G	20	+3	23	+6	29	*Elected*
MR. R	17	+3	20	+4	24	
MR. H	9	−9	0	0	0	
MR. B	11	11	11	−11	0	
Untransferable		3	3	1	4	
Total	57		57		57	
Majority 29	No one elected. Mr. H's votes must be transferred.		No one elected. Mr. B's votes must be transferred.		Majority for Mr. G	

E. Electing a Board by Plurality Vote

When several members are to be elected to a board or council or committee, the desired result can easily be obtained by requiring each voter to vote for just the number to be elected. For example, if 5 members are to be elected from a list of 13, the voter would simply put a cross after each of five names that he might select. Then, when the votes are counted, the 5 candidates who received the *highest number of votes* are declared elected. This method of voting is satisfactory only if each person elected has received a majority of the votes cast, a result that is possible if the number of candidates does not greatly exceed the number of places to be filled. If the number of candidates is much greater than the number to be elected, however, as in the illustration given above where there are 13 candidates from which only 5 are to be elected, some of those elected under this plan will have, not a majority of votes, but a *plurality* only. Election by plurality is permissible only when authorized by the Bylaws. (Cf. pp. 60, 61.)

F. Electing a Board by Preferential Ballot

If the Bylaws of an organization require that each board member be elected *by a majority of the votes,* the *preferential ballot* or *single transferable vote* should be used, as explained on pages 62 et seq.; i.e., all candidates on the ticket should be ranked 1st choice, 2nd choice, 3rd choice, 4th choice, and so on.

The ballots, when received by the tellers, could be treated and tabulated in the manner explained under Preferential Ballot, pp. 62 et seq.; i.e., if, on the first choice, any candidate has a majority of *firsts,* he is declared elected; then the lowest candidate in the list is dropped, and the votes of this candidate are transferred to the candidates marked 2nd choice on his ballots, and so on until 5 members have been elected, each by a majority of the votes cast.

A simpler way, however, is shown on pp. 66, 67, 68. The tellers could list all the numbers received by each candidate and then average these numbers. The candidate with the highest average (smallest figure) would be the first elected; the one with the second highest average (2nd smallest figure) would be the second candidate elected, and so on until 5, the required number, have been elected. If all candidates have received the same number of votes, averaging is unnecessary; then the candidate receiving the smallest total of points is the first one elected, the one receiving the second smallest total of points is the second one elected, and so on.

If five members are to be elected and the 5th and the 6th are tied, the candidate with the larger number of *firsts* should be given the preference, or, if neither has any *firsts,* the candidate with the larger number of *seconds* should be declared the winner, and so on.

Even before the averages are made, certain results may be obvious to the tellers at a glance; e.g., if a candidate has a majority of *firsts,* he should be declared elected regardless of his total or average; if, in a list of 13 candidates, a person has no vote or very few votes smaller than 12 or 13, he is definitely *not* elected; if he has no vote smaller than 6 (where 5 are to be elected), he is *not* elected. To be elected as

TALLY SHEET

Number of ballots cast: ~~THL THL THL THL THL~~
                            ~~THL THL HLL THL THL~~ = 50

For Directors	Votes Received	Total Points	No. of votes rec'd [1]	Average Rank	Elected
RANDOLPH	7-8-7-7-6-7-6-7-7-8-9-7-7 6-9-7-8-7-6-7-7-6-7-6-7 7-10-13-7-1-12-7-11-7-7-6 10-7-7-7-7-6-7-8-6-7-3-13-10-7	369	50	7.38	
BROWN	5-4-6-5-4-6-4-8-5-4-4-5-5 4-3-5-6-5-2-5-5-4-5-4-5 5-9-12-5-3-7-5-4-5-5-4-6 5-1-5-5-5-5-7-4-5-2-12-8-5	275	50	5.50	5
WINSTON	9-10-8-9-8-9-10-9-9-10-8-9 8-8-9-13-9-7-9-9-8-9-8-9-9 8-1-9-4-6-9-3-9-9-8-11-9-2 9-9-10-9-6-10-9-4-11-12-9-9	424	50	8.48	
DARROW	1-1-2-1-7-1-3-1-1-2-1-1-1 2-1-2-1-3-1-1-2-1-1-1-1 1-8-1-2-4-1-2-1-1-1-2-1 5-1-1-1-2-1-3-1-5-10-4-1-1	101	50	2.02	1
STEVENS	10-9-9-10-9-10-9-13-10-9-10-10 11-10-10-12-10-8-10-10-9-10-13-10 10-7-6-10-5-3-10-12-10-10-13-9 10-8-10-10-9-10-4-11-10-6-9-13-10-10	476	50	9.52	
ALLEN	6-6-5-6-5-5-7-5-6-6-7-6-7 7-6-5-6-9-6-6-5-6-7-6-6-5-7-6 11-2-6-13-6-6-7-12-6-9-6-6 7-6-5-8-6-1-8-9-6-6	326	50	6.52	
PRENTISS	4-5-4-4-3-4-5-2-4-5-3-4 5-1-4-4-4-1-4-4-3-4-5-4 4-6-5-4-12-8-4-5-4-4-5-4 4-3-4-4-4-4-3-1-4-7-7-7-4-4	215	50	4.30	4
GOODMAN	8-7-10-8-13-8-8-6-8-7-6-8 9-6-8-7-8-10-8-8-7-8-9-8-8 4-3-8-13-9-8-1-8-8-9-7-8-11 8-8-11-8-2-9-8-10-6-11-8-8	395	50	7.90	
CARTER	2-3-1-2-1-3-1-3-2-1-5-2 2-4-2-3-2-4-2-2-1-2-2-2 2-3-2-2-10-10-2-6-2-2-3-8 2-6-2-2-3-1-2-2-2-9-1-5-2-2	147	50	2.94	2

[1] If all candidates have the same number of votes, as in this case, averaging is unnecessary.

LAWRENCE	3-2-3-3-2-2-4-3-3-2-3 3-5-3-1-3-5-3-3-13-3-3-3 12-9-3-9-1-3-7-3-3-2-5-3 4-3-3-2-3-4-7-3-8-2-6-3-3	194	50	3.88	3
MILLER	13-11-12-13-12-11-13-12-13-13-13-13 13-12-11-13-11-13-11-13-13-12-13-11 13-13-2-10-13-8-5-13-8-13-13-12-13 3-13-12-13-13-13-13-13-11-12-13-12-3-3				
KNIGHT	12-13-11-12-11-13-12-11-12-11-11-12 13-12-12-10-12-13-12-11-11-12-12-12 12-11-4-12-7-11-12-9-12-12-11-13-12 13-12-12-12-12-5-10-12-11-4-1-12-12				
FREEMAN	11-12-13-11-10-12-11-10-11-12-12-11 10-13-11-9-11-12-11-12-10-11-10-11 11-13-11-11-6-13-11-10-11-11-10-1 11-10-11-1-8-11-9-13-11-3-5-2-11-11				

one of 5 candidates, a person must have some votes of 5 or less. When the number of candidates far exceeds the number to be elected, the tellers, in tallying the votes received, will save time and simplify their work by striking out the names of those candidates who obviously and undoubtedly have no prospect of election because their average or total number of rank-points will be much too large.

Thus, in the illustration above, it is obvious from the tally sheet that MR. MILLER, MR. KNIGHT, and MR. FREEMAN have no chance of election and that their votes do not need to be totaled or averaged. It was obvious also before averaging or totaling that MR. STEVENS and even MR. WINSTON had no chance of being elected. The votes of the remaining eight candidates, however, would have to be totaled and, if the number of votes were not the same for each candidate, would have to be averaged.

If, in marking their ballots, *some* voters have not followed directions and have not marked *all* the candidates, it is absolutely necessary to average the votes, since the divisor, i.e., the total number of rank-points, will not be the same for all. If *many* of the voters have failed to rank all candidates, there may be difficulties in determining the outcome of the election. The tellers, in such cases, should bear in mind that the average of a small number of votes is not comparable with the same average of a large number.

Candidate	Votes received	Total	No. of votes received	Average	Elected
MR. A	1-1-1-1-1-1-1 1-1-1-1-1-1-1	14	14	1.	
MR. B	1-1-1-2-3-4-5 1-1-1-1-1-2-2 1-1-2-2-1-1-1 1-1-1-1-1-1-1 1-1-1-1-1-1-1 2-2-2-1-1-2-2 2-1-1-4-2-3-1 1	73	50	1.46	X

In the illustration given here MR. B is the first choice of more than half of the voters (50) and is therefore elected over MR. A, who has a higher average. MR. A is the first choice of only 14 of the 50 members. The other 36 members who did not vote for him may have refused to consider him for any position on the board, and all but 3 of them voted for MR. B. The rules governing election by this method should emphasize the importance of ranking *all* candidates on the ballot and should specify the minimum number of votes that a candidate must receive in order to be considered among the winners.

G. Absentee Voting by Proxy

A proxy is a written authorization of an absentee member conveying to a particular member in attendance the power to cast the vote of the former, as in the case of an election of officers or directors in a stock corporation. Voting by proxy is improper in deliberative assemblies; it is illegal in municipal, state, and national elections; and it is undesirable in most social, religious, or benevolent societies. It is impossible and out of order anywhere unless it is specifically provided for in the Bylaws or standing rules, or unless by a majority vote it is authorized to be used at a specific time or with reference to a particular subject. If, however, a state law empowers members of a corporation to vote by proxy, that right cannot be denied to a member by the Bylaws, rules, or votes of a society.

H. Proportional Representation

If a large organization is made up of elected representatives from various smaller groups or voting units, the Bylaws of the larger organization will specify the basis of representation, the number of representatives allotted to each unit, and, possibly, how they are to be elected. Each unit, however, will conduct its own elections and select its own representatives. In such a situation it is easy to have each constituent group represented according to its size and importance.

Difficulty is encountered, however, when a large organization merely comprises groups or blocs of persons of different party affiliations or interests and it is desirable, in making up a council or board or committee, to have each party or bloc or interest represented in proportion to its strength so that the council, board, or committee will be a true cross-section of the entire organization. The most satisfactory system that has been devised for meeting such a situation is the Hare System [1] of Proportional Representation.

This system employs the preferential ballot or single transferable vote, explained on pp. 62–64. For example, suppose that the ballot contains the names of 12 candidates for 5 positions on a board and that each voter, according to instructions, has marked his 1st choice, 2nd choice, 3rd choice, 4th choice, 5th choice, and no more. The ballots, when collected by the tellers, are stacked in piles, according to 1st choices, and are then counted. Suppose that the results are as follows:

Mr. STEWART 17		Mr. MORRIS 12
Mr. PERRY 7		Mr. HARPER 15
Mr. WARNER 39		Mr. DAVIS 2
Mr. JACKSON 8		Mr. KENNEDY 7
Mr. FOSTER 4		Mr. RUSSELL 20
Mr. CLARK 9		Mr. NELSON 10
Total votes cast 150			

Each candidate, according to the principle of proportional representation, needs for election only a *quota* or *proportionate part* of the total number of votes cast; e.g., if 150 votes are cast for 5 candidates, each candidate would logically need only ⅕ of 150, or 30 votes.[2] In the illustration given above, MR. WARNER, with 39 votes, has passed the required quota on the first choice and is therefore declared elected. His surplus of 9 votes will now be distributed in the following manner: 9 ballots—preferably the last 9 counted—will be removed from his pile and transferred to the candidate marked "2nd choice" on those ballots. If more than one candidate has been elected on the 1st choice, each one's surplus—if there is a surplus—will be transferred

[1] Originated by Thomas Hare, an English political reformer (1806–1891).
[2] According to the original Hare system the quota was determined by dividing the total number of votes by the number of places to be filled plus one and then adding one. Thus in the example above the quota would have been 26 [(150 ÷ 6) + 1].

Candidates	1st Choice	Transfer of Warner's surplus	Result	Transfer of Davis's votes	Result	Transfer of Foster's votes	Result	Transfer of Perry's votes
STEWART	17	+2	19	+1	20		20	+2
PERRY	7		7		7		7	−7
WARNER	39	−9	30		30		30	
JACKSON	8		8		8		8	
FOSTER	4		4		4	−4	0	
CLARK	9		9		9		9	
MORRIS	12	+3	15		15		15	
HARPER	15	+1	16	+1	17	+3	20	+2
DAVIS	2		2	−2	0		0	
KENNEDY	7		7		7		7	
RUSSELL	20	+3	23		23	+1	24	+3
NELSON	10		10		10		10	
Total	150							

in like manner. Next, the candidate who has the lowest number of votes is dropped from the list, and his votes are transferred to the candidate marked "2nd choice" on his ballots. If any candidate now has the required quota, he is declared elected. Again the lowest candidate is eliminated, and his votes are transferred.[1]

Now again, if any one of the surviving candidates has a quota of votes, he is declared elected. The procedure is repeated until the required number of candidates has been elected. While it is possible

---

[1] If on any ballot the candidate marked "2nd choice" has already been eliminated, the vote cannot be transferred. If votes are to be transferred to a 2nd choice and this 2nd choice has already been elected, they should be given to the 3rd choice. If only a part of the votes is needed to elect the 2nd choice, the excess votes should be given to the 3rd choice, except on the final transfer, where they will be added to the quota already received.

Result	Transfer of Kennedy's votes	Result	Transfer of Jackson's votes	Result	Transfer of Clark's votes	Result	Transfer of Nelson's votes	Result	ELECTED
22	+1	23	+7	30		30	+1	31	X
0		0		0		0		0	
30		30		30		30	+2	32	X
8		8	−8	0		0			
0		0		0		0			
9		9		9	−9	0			
15		15		15	+5	20	+6	26	X
22	+3	25	+1	26	+4	30	+1	31	X
0		0		0		0		0	
7	−7	0		0		0		0	
27	+3	30		30		30		30	X
10		10		10		10	−10	0	

that, after the transfer of votes, still no candidate has a quota, it is also possible that two or more candidates may reach the quota at the same time. The final candidate may be declared elected even if he does not have a quota, provided that he has more votes than any other surviving candidate. The details of this plan of voting are illustrated in the chart above.

Chapter XII

SECRETARIES

A. Recording Secretary or Clerk

The duties of the Recording Secretary are these:

1. To keep a register of members.
2. To call the roll of members at the beginning of a meeting when instructed by the presiding officer to do so, and to keep a record of attendance and absence of members.
3. To call the roll when a vote is taken by *yeas* and *nays*.
4. To read the minutes of the last previous meeting. (He should stand to do so.)
5. To keep a record of the proceedings of meetings (see Minutes) and sign his name to such records.
6. To count the votes when a "division" is ordered, i.e. when a vote is required by standing or by raising hands. In large assemblies the counting may be done by tellers appointed by the chairman.
7. To see that appointed committee members are notified of their appointment and their duties, according to the record.
8. To keep on hand at each meeting a copy of the following for ready reference of the chairman:
    a. A list of the members on each committee.
    b. A copy of the Constitution, Bylaws, and Standing Rules, a list of the officers, and a list of the committees of the organization.
    c. Written communications that are to be considered at the meeting.
    d. The complete agenda of the meeting; i.e. the items of business which, according to the record, are to be considered at the meeting.
9. To prepare the agenda (i.e. the list of things to be done) for the next meeting and, if instructed by the assembly or required by the Bylaws to do so, to send a copy of the agenda

with a notice of the time and place of meeting to each member prior to the date of meeting.

10. To furnish delegates with credentials.

11. To draw and sign, along with the President, all vouchers or warrants upon the Treasurer.

12. To preserve and safeguard the Constitution, Bylaws, Standing Rules, the Minutes, and other records; to file and keep all documents of the society, all reports, and all other papers delivered to his custody. No other person, except the President, shall, without authorization of the society, have access to the place in which the records are kept.

13. To perform any other duties assigned to him by the Bylaws or the action of the organization.

14. To prepare ballots for elections.

15. To call a meeting to order if both the President and the Vice-President (or Vice-Presidents, if there are two or more) should be absent, and in such case to entertain a motion for the election of a temporary chairman.

In the absence of the regular secretary, the chairman should appoint a temporary secretary. Such an appointee serves only for the one occasion (*pro tempore*) and, upon adjournment of the meeting, delivers his records to the regular secretary or to the president. Such temporary appointment does not constitute membership on any committee or board to which the regular secretary may belong *ex officio*.

The secretary of an organization, of course, does not function as the secretary of any subdivision of an organization. A committee or board should have its own secretary and keep a record of its own proceedings. The minutes of such units are distinct and separate from the minutes of the society as a whole.

B. The Clerk's (Recording Secretary's) Record

The Clerk, or Recording Secretary, should have two permanent books, as follows:

1. The Journal, which will have numbered pages and will contain—
   a. The list of members.
   b. The minutes of all meetings after they have been approved by the society. They should be arranged in chronological order.
   c. References to the places in which are filed the reports, papers, communications, and other records of the society.

    d. An alphabetical index for quick reference. This may need frequent revisions.

2. A separate book containing the Constitution, Bylaws, and Standing Rules written only on alternate pages. Amendments, if any are adopted, having first been recorded in the Minutes, may then be entered on the blank pages of this book directly opposite the articles to which they pertain, with a notation of the date of adoption and a reference to the page of the Minutes containing the record.

The Recording Secretary's records are, at suitable times, open to inspection by members at the Secretary's convenience and under his supervision.

C. Other Secretaries

Large organizations, if extensive correspondence is required, may find it advisable to have a *Corresponding Secretary* in addition to a Recording Secretary. Sometimes a *Financial Secretary* also is needed. If such officers are required, their duties should be specifically set forth and clearly defined in the Bylaws.

An *Executive Secretary* is a salaried, full-time officer and general manager employed by the Executive Committee of the Board of Directors to see that orders are carried out. He is usually *ex officio* secretary of the Executive Committee, in its name conducts all business between meetings of the Committee, and prepares the Annual Report, which, when adopted by the Committee, is submitted by the Committee to the Board of Directors for approval, and by the Board to the convention.

Chapter XIII

THE MINUTES (RECORD, JOURNAL)

The Minutes (also called The Record or The Journal), which are the record of the proceedings of a society, are intended for the information and guidance of the members and officers.

A. What the Minutes Should Contain

The record of proceedings should contain the following:

1. The name of the society or club.
2. The date and place of meeting.
3. The kind of meeting (i.e., whether *regular* or *special, adjourned regular* or *adjourned special*).
4. The purpose of the meeting, if the meeting was specially called.
5. The hour of calling the meeting to order.
6. The name of the presiding officer.
7. The name of the secretary if he was a substitute for the regular secretary.
8. The names of members present and of those absent (especially in small organizations) or merely the number of members present (the usual practice when an assembly is large). The former practice implies that the roll was called.
9. A statement that the minutes of the last previous meeting were read and approved, or approved without reading (as might be the case if they had previously been mimeographed and distributed), or were not read at all.
10. All main motions that were made and not withdrawn, and whether they were carried or lost, referred to a committee, postponed, or laid "on the table." The motions should be in the exact words of those who made them.
11. All subsidiary motions adhering to the main motion if the main motion is passed.
12. All written reports in full. If a report is long, it should be filed, and the Minutes should contain a reference to that effect along

with a very brief statement (in the language of the Secretary) of its nature or substance.

13. The number of affirmative and the number of negative votes when voting by *yeas* and *nays* has been ordered. The vote of each member should be recorded after his name on a membership roll.

14. If no formal action of any kind is taken at a meeting, the Minutes should state the fact and merely mention that there was discussion of certain matters. (See B-4, below.)

15. The manner and the exact time of adjournment.

16. The Secretary's signature. (When the Minutes are published, the President's name also should be subscribed.)

Each motion made and the outcome of the vote on it should be put in a separate paragraph. (See pp. 77–79.)

B. What the Minutes Should Not Contain

The following cautions should be observed in writing the Minutes:

1. The Minutes should *not* be written as an essay or newspaper article.

2. They should *not* contain the opinion of the Secretary.

3. They should *not* contain any personal comments of the Secretary.

4. They should *not* record what was said in the discussion of motions. (See A-14, above.)

5. They should *not* contain the Minutes of boards or committees.

6. They should *not* contain incidental motions (see pp. 34–39) that are of no consequence to the society and of no effect upon the outcome of the vote on the main motion.

7. If a main motion is lost, the subsidiary motions that were adhering to it are omitted.

8. If a main motion is lost, it may be struck from the *notes* of the Secretary but should *not* be *erased,* since there must be a record of its defeat to refer to in case of an attempt to renew it. (It would be best for the Secretary to keep his original notes taken during the meeting.) In the reading of the Secretary's Minutes at the next meeting, however, and in the permanent record book there need not be a reference to the lost motion, unless the rules of the society so require.

C. Model of Minutes

(See Model Meeting I, pp. 122–125.)

JEFFERSON CIVIC CLUB
Regular Monthly Meeting of
Feb. 9, 1953

Held in the Club Rooms in Emerson Hall

The meeting was called to order by the President, MR. J——, at 7:45 P.M.

Number of members present 125

Members absent: (their names) . . . .

. . . .

. . . .

The Minutes of the regular meeting of Jan. 10, 1953, were read by the Secretary. They were corrected and approved as corrected.

The Treasurer's report was read by the Treasurer, MR. D.

It was moved by MR. E to accept the report.

The Auditor's report, on file, was read by the Secretary.

The Treasurer's report was found to be correct.

MR. E's motion to accept the Treasurer's report was carried.

A copy of the Treasurer's report was received by the Secretary and filed with the Auditor's report (Journal, p. —).

Reports of Standing Committees

1. The report of the Legislative Committee was read by MR. H, the chairman.

    MR. J moved to adopt it.   The motion was carried.

    A copy of the report was delivered to the Secretary and filed (Journal, p. —).

2. The report of the Publicity Committee was read by MR. ——, chairman.

    MR. X moved to adopt the report.

    The motion was carried.

    A copy of the report was delivered to the Secretary and filed (Journal, p. —).

3. The report of the Membership Committee was read by MR. ——, chairman.

    It was moved by MR. —— to adopt the report.

    The motion was carried.

    A copy of the report was delivered to the Secretary and filed (Journal, p. —).

Reports of Special Committees

1. A report of the Committee on Arrangements for the National Convention was read by Mr. ——, chairman.

   It was moved by Mr. —— to accept the report.

   The motion was carried.

   A copy of the report was received by the Secretary and filed (Journal, p. —).

2. The report of the committee appointed to confer with the mayor on the matter of rezoning in Ward No. — was read by Mr. ——, the chairman.

   It was moved by Mr. S to accept the report.   The motion was carried.

   A copy of the report was received by the Secretary and filed (Journal, p. —).

Unfinished Business

It was moved by Mr. M "that the Treasurer and the Directors be instructed and empowered to take the necessary steps to refinance the mortgage at the lowest possible rate."   The motion was carried.

New Business

There was no new business.

Mr. Q moved "to adjourn." The motion was carried.

The meeting was adjourned at 10:45 P.M.

ROBERT H. LOWRY, Secretary.

D. Model Form of Secretary's Notes

The following notes on the proceedings of Model Business Meeting II (see pp. 126–131) were taken by the Secretary while the meeting was in progress.

(*Note*: The first part of the meeting having been omitted, the record began with New Business.)

New Business

Moved by R   "that our usual appropriation for delegates be increased this
Sec. by S   year by $150 in order to send an additional delegate to the Nat'l Convention in N. Y. City."

Moved by T   "to amend by inserting the words 'or more if necessary'
Sec. by U   after the figure $150."

Moved by V   "to amend the amendment by inserting the words 'the Club
Sec. by W   considers it' between the words 'if' and 'necessary,' so that the amendment will read 'if the Club considers it necessary.' "

Moved by A *Sec. by* B	"to refer R's motion to a committee of 3 to be appointed by the Chair."	
Moved by C *Sec. by* D	"that R's motion be postponed until our next regular meet-ing."	
Moved by F *Sec. by* G	"to lay motion on the table."	*—Lost*
Moved by J *Sec. by* K	"that debate on this question ("to postpone R's motion") be closed."	*—Carried*
	C's motion "to postpone" is	*—Lost*
	A's motion "to commit" is	*—Lost*
	V's motion "to amend the amendment" is	*—Carried*
	T's motion "to amend" is	*—Carried*
Moved by N *Sec. by* O	"that the *Previous Question* be ordered on R's motion."	*—Carried*
	R's motion is	*—Carried*
Moved by P *Sec. by* Q	"that we take a recess of an hour."	*—Carried*

Meeting recessed at . . . . . .

ROBERT H. LOWRY, Sec.

E. The Minutes of Model Business Meeting II

(Pages 126–131.)

—as written from the Secretary's notes (pp. 78–79) taken at the meeting and as put in proper form for reading at the next meeting and for final recording (when approved) in the Journal:

(Everything omitted up to New Business)

New Business

It was moved by MR. R "that our usual appropriation for delegates be increased this year by $150 in order to send an additional delegate to the National Convention in New York City."

It was moved by MR. T "to amend the motion by inserting the words 'or more if necessary' after the figure $150."

MR. V moved "to amend the amendment by inserting the words 'the Club considers it' between the words 'if' and 'necessary,' so that the amendment will read 'if the Club considers it necessary.' "

MR. V's and MR. T's amendments were both passed, and MR. R's original motion, as amended, was carried.

Upon a motion by MR. P, the Club was recessed at . . . o'clock for one hour.

ROBERT H. LOWRY, Secretary

F. Model of Minutes

 —of a meeting of which, because of a lack of particular motions, a summary of proceedings is necessary:

THE JEFFERSON FORENSIC CLUB
Special Meeting of
May 16, 1953
Held in the Club Rooms in Prentiss Hall

The meeting was called to order at 8 P.M by the President, MR. J.
  Number of members present 120
  Members absent: (their names) . . . .
   . . . .
   . . . .
   . . . .

The purpose of the meeting was to discuss ways of improving the quality of Club programs.

The President reported his own observations and the criticisms that he had heard.

Informal discussion brought out the following defects in the programs:

1. Subjects have been too difficult.

2. Speeches have often been of poor quality, because of—
 a. Lack of preparation.
 b. Lack of training in—
  (1) English composition;
  (2) Speech organization;
  (3) Oral delivery.

3. Program debates have too often shown a lack of skill in—
 a. Analysis of the question;
 b. Discovering the issues involved;
 c. Formal proof and the use of evidence;
 d. Detecting and refuting fallacies;
 e. Using authorities and sources.

The point was made that the Club critics, although they are required to criticize such defects and make suggestions for correction and improvement, cannot possibly give the needed assistance in the brief time allowed at each meeting for their reports.

It seemed to be the consensus of the Club that, if these faults are to be corrected, it would be advisable for the Club to—

1. Employ an experienced coach qualified to give expert counsel and assistance in the matters referred to above; and

2. To require each assigned speaker to report to the coach for criticism of MS, instruction in delivery, and training in other matters as needed before appearing on the program.

It was voted to make the matter a special issue at the next regular meeting. The meeting was adjourned at 10 P.M.

ROBERT H. LOWRY, Secretary

G. Speed in Taking Minutes

Speed may be important to a secretary. A clerk who is a stenographer can easily keep up with the proceedings in any business meeting, but one who must take notes in longhand may frequently fall behind. When the tempo becomes too fast, the secretary should not hesitate to ask the chairman for help. The record of proceedings is so important that it is justifiable to interrupt, if necessary, at any juncture in order to verify a point. The chairman, if he is experienced, will know what a reasonable tempo is and will regulate his speed accordingly. He will frequently glance at the clerk to see whether help is needed and, if the clerk is seated nearby, as he should be, may even inspect the record for errors now and then. However, when the chairman is busily occupied and the action of the meeting becomes confused or too fast for recording, the clerk should address the Chair and request a precise statement of what happened.

Chapter XIV

TREASURER

A. Duties of Treasurer

The Treasurer of a society holds the funds delivered to him and, upon warrants signed by the President and the Secretary, disburses the money on demand. He must be prepared to give a formal report on receipts and disbursements at the intervals fixed in the Bylaws and at any other times set by the vote or the custom of the society.

B. Treasurer's Reports

All societies require a comprehensive annual report at the end of the fiscal year, some also require a report at the end of each quarter, and in some a monthly report is common. Such reports, after they are presented, should be referred to the Board of Auditors for examination. If there is no Board of Auditors, an auditing committee should be appointed to verify the report. The auditors, if no error has been found in the Treasurer's report, certify to its correctness by signing a statement to that effect at the bottom of the report and deliver the certified report to the President. A vote is then taken on the Auditor's report, approval of which is also approval of the Treasurer's report. The following model will serve as an illustration of the form commonly used in a Treasurer's report:

JEFFERSON FORENSIC CLUB

Report of the Treasurer for the quarter ending March 31, 1953.
Balance in the treasury on Jan. 1, 1953 . . . . . . $ 65.50

Receipts

Initiation fees	$ 10.00	
Members' dues	225.00	
Fines	9.00	. . . $244.00
Total		. $309.50

Disbursements

Rent of hall—3 months	$135.00	
Electricity	12.00	
Stationery	6.50	

Mimeographing and printing . . .	8.00	
Postage	9.50	
Janitor service	30.00	$201.00
Balance on hand March 31, 1953		108.50
Total		. $309.50

WILLIAM H. HARPER
Treasurer
Submitted March 31, 1953

Examined and found correct
March 31, 1953 by
ROBERT J. RANDOLPH ⎱
JOHN W. STEVENS ⎰ Auditing Committee

C. Treasurer's Vouchers

All bills to be paid by the Treasurer must first be approved by a vote of the assembly. The Minutes will record that they were allowed, and the Secretary will issue an "order to pay," signed by himself and the President. In the case of a statement for materials or service the simplest procedure is to stamp the bills thus:

Payment authorized.   Date _____

Signed: _____ President

_____ Secretary

For other disbursements it would be best to have printed or mimeographed warrants similar to the following:

No. _____   Date _____

THE JEFFERSON FORENSIC CLUB

authorizes the Treasurer of the Club to pay

Amount _____ $ _____

To _____

For _____

Signed: _____ President

_____ Secretary

Chapter XV

BOARDS

A large organization that meets only annually or quarterly usually elects a Board of Managers or Directors to conduct its affairs between meetings. Such a Board elects its own secretary, has its own Bylaws, which are subordinate to and governed by the rules of the parent body, and meets monthly or quarterly.

It appoints or elects from its own membership a small Executive Committee to manage the affairs of the Board between Board meetings. Sometimes a Board is subdivided into committees, each of which is responsible for some particular activity of the organization during the interval between Board meetings. If an organization is large, the Executive Committee holds frequent regular or special meetings and employs a full-time general manager known as the Executive Secretary of the organization, who is *ex officio* Secretary of the Executive Committee and usually of the Board. (See p. 74.) The Executive Committee is responsible to the Board of Directors or Managers, which, in turn, is responsible to the parent society.

Although all members of a Board are elected for terms of the same length, they should not all be elected at the same time. If it is provided in the Bylaws of the society that one third of the members go out of office each year and an equal number of new members be elected to take their places, two thirds of the Board would always be experienced or "holdover" members. In such a case, even though only one third of the members are new, the Board is regarded as a new Board, and new officers and committees are elected for the ensuing year. Unfinished business left over from the year just closed is not carried over to the new year.

If a Board is large, its business is transacted in the same formal manner as in meetings of the parent society or any other large organization. (See pp. 122–167.)

A Board is usually required by the Bylaws of an organization to make an annual report to the parent society at the annual meeting. It is customary for such a report to give a review of the activities of the Board for the twelve months just ended and to make recommendations for the future. The report, when discussed and adopted, may be published in the annual proceedings of the society. If amendments have been made, they must be indicated as such by the use of brackets around the words to be struck out and by italics for the words that have been added, the original text being intact.

Sometimes certain persons have places on the Board by virtue of the offices to which they have been elected or which they have been employed to fill. These are called *ex officio* members. When they go out of office, their connection with the Board is automatically terminated. While they are in office and are functioning with the Board, they have the same standing as other members, are counted in a quorum, and have the right to vote. The president, however, unless he has been explicitly so designated, is not regarded as a member of the Board, even though he may be permitted to attend its meetings.

Chapter XVI

COMMITTEES

Much of the work of large assemblies is done by committees, i.e., small groups of members either elected by the organization or appointed by the chairman, with the authorization of the assembly, for the purpose of performing some definite task. In deliberative bodies the matters to be discussed are usually prepared and introduced by committees.

A. "Standing" Committees

—are those specifically named in the Bylaws and regularly elected or appointed for definite terms to perform particular assignments of a permanent nature. Such are the Executive Committee, the Finance Committee, the Ways and Means Committee, the Public Relations Committee, the Program Committee, the Legislative Committee, and certain others. (Cf. p. 108.) "Standing" Committees, especially if they are large, usually elect a secretary to keep a record of the proceedings.

B. Special Committees

—are those which, when a need arises, are elected or appointed in accordance with the vote of an assembly to render a particular service of temporary character. They cease to exist as soon as they have performed the assignments given them and have made acceptable reports or are discharged by a vote of the assembly. If a committee gives an unsatisfactory report, the question may be *re*committed for further study or referred to a new committee.

If the person making the motion that authorizes the appointment of a special committee does not specify who the chairman is to be and if no one of the appointed members is named as chairman, the member first appointed is the chairman. In his absence the next named person becomes chairman, and so on unless the committee elects its chairman, as it has the right to do.

The presiding officer of an assembly, when authorized to appoint a committee, often includes the member who made the motion and designates him as chairman. The Chair, however, should not assume that the maker of the motion is bidding for the chairmanship of the committee or that he is the person best qualified for the position.

A committee that is intended to carry out some course of action should be small and should be composed of persons favorable to the proposed action. On the other hand, if a committee is selected only for deliberation on the investigation of some problem, it should be large and should include representative members of all the factions or interest groups in the organization.

It is generally desirable that a committee have an odd number of members in order to prevent tie votes.

C. Committees—Chairmen and Meetings

A committee should assemble at the call of its chairman or at the summons of any two other members if the chairman is disinclined or unable to perform his duty.

In large committees a secretary should be elected. If a special committee is small, however, no secretary is needed; the chairman himself will keep the necessary memoranda for a report.

A committee may hold hearings upon the question referred to it, inviting members to be present and to give their views, and it *must* do so upon demand of members. Non-members, however, are not permitted to remain in the meeting during the deliberations of the committee.

The several meetings of a special committee constitute a session.

D. Committees—Selecting a Meeting Date

If a committee is large and its members are scattered over a wide area, it is sometimes difficult for the chairman to set a meeting date suitable to all. In such a case, especially if it is necessary to have several meetings, a chart as on p. 88, filled out by each member of the committee, may be useful in getting a consensus.

E. Procedure in Committee Meetings

The procedure in committee meetings is more informal than in the meetings of a society, and for a small committee, just as in the case of other groups, it is more informal than for a large one. In all committee meetings, however, the general rules of procedure apply, with the following modifications:

1. A quorum is a majority of the members.
2. Motions need not be seconded.
3. Motions to limit or close debate are out of order.
4. If a committee is small, speakers are not required to rise and address the Chair. If more than one should start to speak simultaneously, precedence is decided by the rules of courtesy. If necessary, the Chair decides who has "the floor."

PUBLIC RELATIONS COMMITTEE
of the
HAMILTON CIVIC CLUB

Which day of the week, which day of the month, and what hour of the day would be most suitable for the meetings of the committee? Put a check ($\sqrt{}$) in the column and box indicating your *preference,* a cross ($\times$) in the column and box indicating your *second* choice, and a circle ($\bigcirc$) in the column and box showing your *third* choice. Sign your name at the bottom and deliver this paper to the chairman—

H. W. WHITMAN

APRIL

Hour	Mon.				Tues.				Wed.				Thu.				Fri.				Sat.			
P.M.	1	2	3	4	1	2	3	4	1	2	3	4	1	2	3	4	1	2	3	4	1	2	3	4
3:00																								
4:00																								
5:00																								
6:00																								
7:00																								
8:00																								

Comment—

Signature: _____

5. Each member has the right to speak as many times as he desires.

6. The chairman may participate freely in the discussion or make a motion, and in neither case does he leave his chair to do so.

7. If a committee is small, the chairman does not rise to put the question.

8. Unless settled by general consent (p. 51), all questions must be put to a vote.

9. A vote may be reconsidered at any time upon demand, and the reconsideration may be repeated.

10. A reconsideration may be moved by anyone who did not vote with the losing side, even by a person who was absent when the vote was previously taken.

11. A motion "to reconsider" requires a ⅔ vote unless (a) previous notice has been given to all members, or (b) those who voted on the prevailing side are all present.

12. When a committee has completed its task, it is in order to move "that the committee now rise and that the chairman (or other designated member) make our report to the assembly."

If there are amendments adhering to a question when it is referred to a committee, the committee will consider these and in its report either (a) will recommend that they be adopted or rejected, or (b) will make no recommendation, giving reasons.

If a committee, in its report, recommends amendments to a paper or resolution referred to the committee, these amendments should be written on separate paper.

A committee, in making its report, reveals not the incidents or occurrences in its meetings but merely the outcome of its deliberations, and it reports only the matters agreed upon by the committee in its meetings and designated there for its report. The substance of the report must be authorized by a majority of the committee members present, all members having received previous notice of the meeting.

F. Forms of Committee Reports

The following models will illustrate the forms of committee reports:

1. *If a committee is instructed merely to obtain information for the use of the assembly:*

"The (or "your") committee appointed to obtain estimates on the cost of decorating the new Conference Room according to specifications, reports that it has received the following bids:

Danielson & Hansen . . . . $350.
Johnson, Mead & Company . . . . . . 325.
Herman Olsen Company . . . . 378.

Respectfully submitted,
A. F. HILTON
W. R. TURNER
J. E. RUSSEL"

2. *If a committee has been appointed to obtain information and
   also make a recommendation:*

   "Your (or "the") committee appointed to obtain estimates
   on the cost of altering the main stairway of the club house
   according to specifications, has received the following bids:

   Carlson Brothers . . . . $295.
   Community Builders . . . . 320.
   Erickson & Lindstrom . . . . 280.
   Werner Nelson . . . . 275.

   "We have ascertained that Werner Nelson, who has made
   the lowest bid, is thoroughly reliable and has a reputation for
   expert workmanship; we therefore recommend that his bid be
   accepted.

   Respectfully submitted,
   A. W. HALE
   C. R. MERRILL
   T. S. DIXON"

3. *If a committee has been appointed and given authority to act
   on behalf of the assembly:*

   "The (or "your") committee authorized to secure suitable
   convention accommodations in one of the leading hotels of this
   city, wishes to report that it has engaged the required number
   of sleeping rooms and conference rooms in the Congress
   Hotel for the last three days of March at a rate 10% lower
   than the regular rate.

   Respectfully submitted,
   J. M. SANDERS
   A. G. FULTON
   F. D. ROTH"

4. *If a committee has been appointed to study a motion referred
   to it and make a recommendation:*

   "The (or "your") committee to which was referred the motion 'that the club employ an instructor in public speaking' has

studied the question carefully and recommends that the motion be carried.

> Respectfully submitted,
> R. W. SNYDER
> H. A. TISDALE
> N. J. DENNISON"

5. *If a committee is called up to report on the progress being made by it:*

(See pp. 150–162)

Committee reports, if they deal with important matters, are signed by all committee members who concur in the report, the chairman's name being first. If the report deals with non-critical material, the chairman, with the authorization of the committee, may sign the report alone. In such a case he should add the word "Chairman" after his signature.

G. Minority Reports

Committee members who do not concur in the report or favor the course of action recommended may express their views in what is called a minority report. The following will serve to illustrate the form of such a report:

"The undersigned, a minority of the committee appointed to consider the motion 'that the club employ an instructor in public speaking,' has considered the question carefully and recommends that the motion be defeated because of the heavy expense that would be involved.

> Respectfully submitted,
> W. A. HUBBARD
> C. H. WOODRUFF"

Such a report is intended for the information of the society, which is under no obligation to hear it. The chairman of an assembly, having noticed that a report has not been signed by all members of the committee or having been told by the committee chairman that there was a strong minority element, may, out of courtesy, call upon the minority to express its views. A minority report, if one is submitted, is in order only during the discussion of the regular report.

If the chairman of a committee is himself one of the minority, he cannot sign the regular committee report. Moreover, the report should be read by someone else, an elected member of the majority.

H. Subcommittees

A committee may subdivide its work, electing subcommittees from its own members to perform specific tasks. A subcommittee, if so authorized by the committee that elected it, may even enlist the aid of persons who are outside of the organization, non-members whose cooperation is necessary to the success of some project. A subcommittee is responsible to and makes its report to the larger committee of which it is a part and never to the society itself. Its meetings are governed by the same rules of procedure as the meetings of other special committees.

I. Ex-Officio Members of Committees and Boards

A person who is a member of a committee or board only by virtue of the office that he holds is called an *ex-officio* member. Thus the treasurer may be an *ex-officio* member of the Finance Committee, if there is such a committee. The president is often considered an *ex-officio* member of committees. Such a member has the right to vote in the committee meetings unless the Bylaws provide otherwise, and, if he has the right to vote, he has the right to be counted in a *quorum.* (Cf. p. 85.)

CHAPTER XVII

QUASI COMMITTEES

A. Committee of the Whole

When an assembly, especially a large one, wishes to discuss a matter informally and with great freedom, the usual practice is to refer the question to a Committee of the Whole. The motion needed for the purpose is as follows:

"I move that the Society (or "Assembly" or "Club") resolve itself (or "go") into a Committee of the Whole for the purpose of considering the question of . . . . . ."

(For the qualifications and precedence of this motion, see Table, VI.)

If the motion is carried, the chairman appoints a member of the assembly to act as the chairman of the committee and to preside at the meeting. The regular secretary of the club may take notes on the proceedings of the committee, but these are not entered in the Minutes of the society.

In a meeting of a Committee of the Whole the following regulations are in effect:

1. A quorum is the same as for the whole assembly.

2. The only motions that are in order are these:
   a. "To amend (the question under consideration)."
   b. "To adopt (the question under consideration)."
   c. "To rise and report" (to the assembly). *This motion cannot be debated or amended.*

3. An appeal from the decision of the Chair is permissible.

4. There is no limit to the length of speeches or to the number of times that a member may speak unless restrictions were imposed by the assembly before going into the Committee of the Whole.

The deliberations of a Committee of the Whole are usually terminated by a motion "to rise and report." If this motion is carried, the president of the organization again takes charge of the meeting, and the committee chairman, who has gone back to his seat, rises and makes his report in the following manner:

"The Committee of the Whole, having considered the question

93

of . . . .
has instructed me to report the motion (or 'resolution') with the
following amendments:

    1. . . . .
    2. . . . .";

or "to report the motion without amendments"; *or* "to report that
no conclusion was reached."

The question under discussion is then voted upon by the assembly
without further delay, the amendments being voted upon first, if there
are any.

B. Informal Discussion

If an assembly that is not large desires to discuss a matter informally and with great freedom, the usual practice is, not to go into a
Committee of the Whole, but to adopt a motion like the following:

"I move that we (or "the Club" or "the Assembly" or "the Society") consider informally the question of . . . . . ."

    or

"I move that the question of . . . . . . be considered
informally."

(For qualifications and precedence of this motion, see Table, VI.)

In connection with this motion the following regulations should be
observed:

1. The informality of discussion applies only to the main question
   and any amendments made to it before or after the adoption
   of the motion "to consider informally."

2. The Assembly may, by a ⅔ vote, limit the number and length
   of speeches, or it may close the debate.

3. Unless some restriction has been imposed by a ⅔ vote, any
   member may speak on the question as often as he can get "the
   floor," but preference must be given to a member who has not
   spoken at all on the question.

4. When a vote is taken at the close of an informal consideration,
   it is taken in the usual formal manner.

5. Informal consideration ceases as soon as the main question is
   disposed of by a vote.

CHAPTER XVIII

ORGANIZATION—MASS MEETINGS

A. Definition and Purpose of Mass Meetings

Any meeting of an unorganized group of people who have convened for a specific purpose is customarily called a "mass meeting," even though the number of persons attending be small.

The purpose of such a meeting may be—
1. To deal with some issue or matter temporarily demanding attention, or
2. To organize a permanent society or club.

B. Preparation and Preliminary Steps by Sponsors

Those who are responsible for calling a mass meeting will in advance—
1. Decide the time and place of meeting and secure the necessary accommodations.
2. Issue notices of the time, place, and purpose of the meeting to those who should attend or whose attendance is desired. If it is desired to invite all persons of certain qualifications and the number is large, the call may be broadcast by a newspaper advertisement or radio announcement. If a more exclusive group is wanted, the notices may be given personally by word-of-mouth, telephone, telegraph, or printed invitation.
3. Select one of their own number to call the meeting to order when the people have convened.
4. Select one of their own number to explain the purpose of the meeting when called upon to do so.
5. Select someone to prepare resolutions authorizing the meeting to organize a society or club to carry out the purposes (if an organization is the aim). This person may be the same one who explains the purpose of the meeting.
6. Decide whom they should support as a permanent chairman (if a permanent organization is contemplated).

C. Call to Order and Procedure

When the people have assembled and it is time for the meeting to

95

start, the person designated by the sponsors for opening the meeting will step to the platform and assume the role of temporary chairman, as follows:

CHAIRMAN   (*rapping on the table or desk*): Will the meeting please come to order. If there is no objection, the Chair will appoint MR. . . . . . as temporary secretary. (*The secretary takes a seat at a table near the chairman.*) This meeting has been called for the purpose stated in the announcement that you all received. The Chair will call upon MR. C. to give a full statement of those purposes. (*He waits standing while MR. C. comes forward.*)

MR. C: (*Having arrived at the platform*) Mr. Chairman.

CHAIRMAN: MR. C. (*Chairman takes his seat.*)

MR. C: The purposes for which this meeting has been called are these: (1) . . . . . ; (2) . . . . . ; (3) . . . . . (*He explains in full and then takes his seat.*)

CHAIRMAN: Are there any questions or remarks about this statement of objectives?
                    (*Questions are addressed to the chairman and answered by him or referred to MR. C. Then—*)

MR. D: (*Previously selected by the sponsors*) Mr. Chairman.

CHAIRMAN: MR. D.

MR. D: I wish to offer the following resolutions: . . . . . (*he reads them and hands a copy to the secretary.*)[1]

The resolutions are seconded and voted on in the usual manner. (See pp. 160–162.) If they are adopted, provision must next be made for their implementation. If they are aimed at establishing a permanent organization, it will be necessary to appoint (or elect) a committee to draft a constitution and bylaws. However, the sponsors may have a tentative draft ready to submit at this first meeting. In such a case the proposed constitution and bylaws could be read, discussed, and voted upon at once. (For procedure, see pp. 143–145.)

Permission to vote upon a motion to adopt them is granted only to those who can qualify as members. When finally adopted, the constitution should be signed by all members. The chairman may appoint a temporary treasurer to whom members may pay the initiation fee and dues at once. A short recess should be declared (1) to permit members to pay their fees and dues, and (2) to permit

---

[1] See pp. 131, 160.

those who are not members to withdraw from the meeting, if they have not already done so.

If there is not a draft of the proposed constitution and bylaws ready to submit at the first meeting, the meeting will have to be adjourned to a fixed date when such a draft will be ready. At such an adjourned meeting the temporary chairman will still preside, and the business will proceed from the point at which it was interrupted in the first meeting.

If the Constitution and Bylaws have been adopted at the first meeting, the election of officers may be held immediately (after the recess; see above)—

1. If the time permits and it is the will of the members; and

2. If the Bylaws just adopted do not prevent.

When the election is ended, the permanent officers should take office immediately.

D. Procedure—Alternative

The person calling a mass meeting to order (p. 96) may act as chairman only until a temporary chairman has been elected (instead of following the procedure outlined above in Sect. C). He may proceed as follows:

CHAIRMAN   (*rapping on the table or desk*): Will the meeting please come to order. (*The meeting becomes quiet; then——*) I move that MR. B. act as chairman of this meeting.[1]

SOMEONE   (*in the assembly*) : I second the motion.

CHAIRMAN: It has been moved and seconded that MR. B. act as chairman of this meeting. All who are in favor of the motion will please say "Aye." (*They vote.*) All who are opposed will say "No." (*They vote.*) The motion is carried and MR. B. is elected temporary chairman. Will he please take the chair.

              MR. B. *then comes to the platform and conducts the meeting, proceeding as follows:*

CHAIRMAN: The first business to be attended to is the election of a temporary secretary. Are there nominations for this office?

---

[1] Instead of making a nomination himself, he may ask for nominations and, if there are more than one, conduct an election. If candidates are voted upon orally, they are taken in the order given. If the first nominee has a majority of votes, he is declared elected; if not, the next candidate is voted upon in like manner; and so on until a chairman is elected. If desired, the vote may be by secret ballot.

Mr. D: Mr. Chairman.
Chairman: Mr. D.
Mr. D: I move that Mr. R. act as temporary secretary.
Someone: I second the motion.
Chairman: It has been moved and seconded that Mr. R. act as temporary secretary. All who are in favor of the motion will please say "Aye." (*They vote.*) Those who are opposed will say "No." (*They vote.*) The motion is carried. Mr. R. is elected temporary secretary. Will he please come forward.

              The secretary comes forward and takes a seat at a table near the chairman. He secures paper and records the proceedings of the meeting from the beginning. As soon as the secretary is seated—

Chairman: Will someone state the purpose of the meeting.
Mr. C: Mr. Chairman.
Chairman: Mr. C.
Mr. C: The purposes for which this meeting has been called are these: (1) . . . . ; (2) . . . . ; (3) . . . .

(From this point the procedure would not differ from that outlined in Sect. C, above.)

Chapter XIX

CONVENTIONS

If a convention is unorganized, i.e. if it has not yet adopted a constitution and bylaws and has no elected officers, the procedure is, in general, like that of a mass meeting (See pp. 95–98).

If the convention is that of an organized body, the rules of its government and procedure are, supposedly, prescribed in the Constitution and Bylaws. In such a case the procedure is usually as follows:

A. Preparation for the Convention

1. A committee of the organization reserves a suitable hall and makes other necessary arrangements in the city previously decided upon by the society.
2. A committee, usually the Board of Managers or a committee appointed by it, prepares a program and agenda for the convention and, through the Executive Secretary's office, sends a copy to each member of the organization or publishes it in the society's journal.
3. Delegates are elected by the local, constituent bodies and are provided with credentials.
4. Local, constituent bodies, through their own officers or committees appointed for the purpose, secure transportation and hotel accommodations for their delegates.
5. A Credential Committee or Registration Committee, if not already provided for in the Constitution and Bylaws, is appointed for the convention.
6. Boards and committees that are required to report at the convention prepare their reports.
7. A parliamentarian is engaged for the convention.
8. A stenographer is employed to make a verbatim record of everything that is said in the convention meetings.

B. Convention Procedure

1. Delegates meet at the appointed time and place They present their credentials to the Committee on Credentials or Registration,

and each receives a badge entitling him to admission to the meetings.

2. Guards are posted at the doors to keep out intruders.

3. The president of the association calls the meeting to order.

4. Opening exercises are held, if there are any—such as a greeting from the president, a speech of welcome by the mayor of the city or by the president of the society's local chapter acting as host, and a reply by the president of the convention.

5. The report of the Committee on Credentials [1] or Registration, listing accredited delegates (or their alternates), is read from the platform, usually by the Executive Secretary. Convention officials, members of the Board of Directors, and chairmen of the society's standing committees should be included, since they have a right to vote. The report is voted upon.

6. The report of the Program Committee [1] is presented. It is adopted or amended by a majority vote of the convention. Thereafter it can be altered only by a $\frac{2}{3}$ vote.

7. Reports of the officers of the association.

8. Reports of Boards. (See Ch. XV, p. 84)

9. Reports of standing committees.

10. Reports of special committees.

11. General orders and miscellaneous business.

12. New business. One item should be the appointment of a committee to edit and publish the proceedings of the convention and another to decide the place and time of the next convention.

13. Adjournment *sine die.* (See p. 32)

At the beginning of the second meeting of the convention and at each meeting thereafter, the Minutes of the last preceding meeting are read by the secretary and approved by the convention, except that the Minutes of the last meeting of the session, if there is no chance to have them read, may be approved by the Board of Directors or by some committee upon authorization of the convention.

C. Conferences

Meetings of special-interest groups may be held during the intervals between business meetings of a convention. In such group meetings usually there are special programs, consisting of speeches, debates,

---

[1] The Credentials Committee and the Program Committee are continued throughout the convention.

papers, panel discussions, reports on research projects, demonstrations, or other matters of interest to the group. Procedure in such conferences is very informal. Questions from the audience are permitted and even encouraged. The chairman has nothing to do except announce the speakers on the program, recognize those who raise questions from the floor, and steer the discussion. He himself may participate freely in the discussion and take sides on an issue. He is not an elected officer of the convention but merely a person appointed by the Program Committee to preside as a temporary chairman.

Chapter XX

CONSTITUTIONS, BYLAWS, AND STANDING RULES

A. Constitutions—Basic Principles

The basic principles and general character of an unincorporated organization should be set forth in a constitution, containing only the following:

1. The name and purpose of the organization.
2. Membership:
   a. Who may qualify as a member.
   b. How candidates may (in general) be admitted to membership. (Details should be left to the Bylaws.)
3. Officers:
   a. What officers the organization shall have.
   b. How they shall be elected; i.e., whether by ballot or not. (Details of election procedure may be set forth in the Bylaws.)
4. Meetings—the general policy as to
   a. The kind of meetings to be held.
   b. The number and frequency of the meetings (in general).
5. Amendments—how the Constitution may be amended.

A constitution, since it cannot be suspended, should not contain regulations that ordinarily may be suspended. The article on amendments should specifically provide for (a) previous notice of the proposed amendment and (b) a ⅔ or ¾ vote for its adoption.

B. Model Constitution

The following model will serve to illustrate the principles set forth in Sect. A above:

CONSTITUTION
of the
JEFFERSON FORENSIC CLUB

Article I. Name and Purpose

Sect. A—This society shall be known as The Jefferson Forensic Club.

102

Sect. B—Its purpose shall be to provide opportunities for its members to gain experience and develop skill in (1) public speaking and (2) parliamentary usage.

Article II. Membership

Sect. A—*Qualifications for Membership*

1. Any person—man or woman—who is interested in the objectives of The Jefferson Forensic Club may be considered a candidate for membership, provided that he (or she)—
   a. Is of good moral character;
   b. Is at least 21 years of age;
   c. Has at least a high school education; and
   d. Has no handicap or impediment that would prevent him (or her) from participating in the programs and other activities of the Club.
2. Such a candidate, having filed a written application, shall, if approved by the required vote (Sect. B-2), become a member of the Club upon—
   a. Signing the Constitution and Bylaws, and
   b. Paying the initiation fee and the current dues.

Sect. B—*Manner of Election to Membership*

1. Election to membership shall be by ballot.
2. Three negative votes shall be sufficient to reject an applicant for membership.

Sect. C—*Duties of Members*

All members shall, under penalty of fine, take part in the programs as assigned and perform any other duties that may fall to their lot.

Article III—Officers

Sect. A—*Titles*

The officers of this Club shall be a President, a First Vice-President, a Second Vice-President, a Secretary, and a Treasurer.

Sect. B—*Election and Tenure*

The officers shall be nominated from the floor and elected by ballot at the first regular meeting in September and in February. A majority vote shall be necessary to elect. When there is only one nominee for an office, he may be elected by voice. All officers shall take office immediately at the close of the session in which they are elected.

Sect. C—*Eligibility*

Any member of the Club shall be eligible for election to any office, provided that he—

1. Is in good standing;
2. Has been a member of the Club for at least one year immediately prior to the election; and
3. Has not previously held the same office at any time within the two years immediately prior to the election.

Sect. D—*Vacancies of Office*

If any office shall become vacant, the President shall, at the earliest possible date thereafter, order a special election for the purpose of filling such office. The member thus elected shall immediately enter upon his duties and shall hold office until the next regular election.

Sect. E—*Duties of Officers*

1. The *President* shall—
   a. Preside at all meetings of the Club;
   b. Call special meetings at his discretion, subject to the limitations of Art. IV, Sect. C;
   c. Appoint all committees not otherwise provided for;
   d. Make provision for the discharge *pro tempore* of necessary duties of absent or suspended members;
   e. Sign all warrants on the treasury of the Club;
   f. See that the regulations of the Club are enforced;
   g. Carry out assignments and instructions given to him by vote of the Club; and
   h. Perform such other duties as customarily pertain to the office of President.
2. The *First Vice-President* shall be an aide to the President and, in case of the absence or disability of the President, shall *pro tempore* assume and perform the duties of the President.
3. The *Second Vice-President* shall be chairman of the Membership Committee and shall act as presiding officer of the Club in the absence of both the President and the First Vice-President.
4. The *Secretary* shall—
   a. Keep a record of the proceedings of all meetings;
   b. Issue notices of meetings and agenda, after consultation with the President; and
   c. Conduct the correspondence of the Club.
5. The *Treasurer* shall—
   a. Collect all fees and dues;
   b. Render an account each month, or more often if required, of all receipts and expenditures;
   c. Pay the bills of the Club only after approval by a vote of the Club and upon orders or warrants signed by the President.

Article IV—Meetings

Sect. A—*Time and Place*

At least two regular meetings shall be held in each month from September to June, inclusive, the place and the hour to be determined by the Club.

Sect. B—*Nature of Meetings*

Each meeting shall consist of two parts:

1. A program meeting, devoted to exercises in public speaking. The program shall consist of—
   a. Prepared speeches on assigned topics;
   b. A debate upon some important question;
   c. Extemporaneous speaking;
   d. Other features, if desired, that are consistent with the objectives of the Club.

The program shall immediately follow the roll-call. Visitors may be admitted to the program meeting.

2. A business meeting, the purposes of which shall be—
   a. To transact the business of the Club;
   b. To hear criticisms of the program;
   c. To get practice and develop skill in parliamentary procedure.

Only members of the Club shall attend the business meeting.

Sect. C—*Special Meetings* may be called by the President of the Club when, after consulting the other elected officers, he is convinced that the need is sufficiently urgent. A special meeting shall be called upon demand of any five (5) members, exclusive of the elected officers, regardless of the wish of the President.

Article V—Quorum

For any meeting of this Club a quorum shall consist of one third (⅓) of the members in good standing.

Article VI—Amendments

Sect. A—This Constitution may be amended at any regular business meeting of the Club by a ⅔ vote of those present and voting, provided that written or printed notice of the proposed amendment has been given to all members at least one week previously.

Sect. B—Bylaws of this Club may be adopted at any regular meeting by a majority vote, provided that previous notice was given. After the Bylaws have been adopted, they shall be amended only in accordance with provisions set forth in the Bylaws themselves.

C. Bylaws—Basic Principles

Bylaws should contain important regulations that may be changed somewhat more easily than the constitution, but still not without previous notice. They must be consistent with the general principles set forth in the Constitution.

D. Model Bylaws

The following model will serve as an illustration of the principles set forth in Sect. C:

BYLAWS
of the
JEFFERSON FORENSIC CLUB
Article I—Fees and Dues

Sect. A—The *initiation fee* shall be two dollars ($2.00). (Cf. Constitution, Art. II, Sect. A, 2, b.)

Sect. B—The *annual dues* shall be five dollars ($5.00), payable in advance at the first meeting in January. Any member who is more than 30 days delinquent in the payment of the annual dues shall be notified in writing. If his dues are unpaid three months after they become due, he shall be declared suspended. If he is still delinquent at the end of six (6) months, his name shall be removed from the roll of members, a warning having been sent him thirty days previously.

Article II—Meetings

Sect. A—*Dates of Meetings*

Regular meetings of the Club shall be held on the first and third Mondays of each month from September to June, inclusive.

Sect. B—*Time of Meetings*

All regular meetings shall be held in the evening.

Sect. C—*Place of Meetings*

At the first meeting in December of each year the President shall appoint a committee to find a suitable hall for holding the meetings of the Club during the following calendar year. The committee shall report not later than the second meeting in December.

Article III—Appointed Officers and Boards

Sect. A—*Sergeant-at-Arms*

At each meeting the President shall appoint a Sergeant-at-Arms, whose duties shall be—

1. To guard the door of the hall, permitting no one to enter during a speech when a program is in session;

2. To assist the President in maintaining order when requested by him to do so;
3. To deliver communications, as required, from and to the President during the progress of meetings;
4. To prevent non-members from entering business meetings;
5. To collect judges' ballots at the close of a debate and deliver them to the President.

The same member shall not be Sergeant-at-Arms at more than three meetings during the year.

Sect. B—*Critics*

There shall be two (2) critics, known as the First Critic and the Second Critic, whose duty it shall be to evaluate critically the program as a whole and the work of each participant. The First Critic shall consider the thought, composition, organization, preparation, and delivery of all productions. The Second Critic shall criticize pronunciation, grammar, usage, and all errors overlooked by the First Critic.

Both critics shall be appointed by the President at the beginning of his term, i.e., at the first meeting in September and at the first meeting in February.

Sect. C—*Censors*

There shall be a Board of Censors consisting of three (3) members appointed by the President at the first meeting in September and the first meeting in February. It shall be the duty of the Censors to levy and collect fines, in the amounts authorized by the Club, for the following, unless acceptable excuses are presented:

1. Absence from roll-call.
2. Non-performance of duty in office.
3. Failure to appear on program when assigned.
4. Disorderly conduct in a meeting of the Club.
5. Frivolous or dilatory parliamentary tactics.
6. Indecorum in debate.
7. Failure of a member of the Program Committee to post his program by the required time.

All fines are payable at once. If they are not paid by the time of the next regular meeting, the offender will be reported by the Censors as suspended, and the member shall be notified in writing. If they are not paid by the time of the second meeting after suspension, the member's name shall be removed from the roll of the Club. A member against whom a fine has been assessed may appeal his case to the Club at any time before he is suspended.

Article IV—Committees

Sect. A—*Membership Committee*

The President, after consultation with the other elected officers, shall, at the second regular meeting of September and the second regular meeting of February, appoint six members who, with the Second Vice-President as chairman (Cf. Constitution, Art. III, Sect. E, 3), shall constitute the Membership Committee. It shall be the duty of this committee (1) to make contacts with persons interested in becoming members of the Club, (2) to examine the qualifications of applicants, and (3) to recommend to the Club suitable candidates for membership.

Sect. B—*Program Committee*

There shall be a Program Committee, consisting of three (3) members, whose duty it shall be to prepare programs for all program meetings. At each regular business meeting the chairman of the committee shall announce the program for the second program meeting thereafter, shall post a typewritten copy of the program in a conspicuous place in the hall, and, on the night of the meeting, shall deliver a copy to the President.

The members of the Program Committee shall be appointed by the President at the second regular meeting of September and the second regular meeting of February after consultation with the other elected officers.

Sect. C—*Auditing Committee*

Annually at the second regular business meeting in January and at the second regular business meeting in June the President shall appoint a committee of three (3) members to audit the Treasurer's and the Censors' books.

Article V—Programs

Sect. A—*General Topic*

All speeches on a regular program shall be related to a general topic or subject field.

Sect. B—*Nature of Programs*

Each regular program shall consist of the following:

1. At least four (4) *prepared speeches* on assigned phases of the general topic, each speech to be not more than eight (8) minutes in length.
2. At least four (4) *extemporaneous speeches* on phases of the general topic, each speech to be not more than four (4) minutes in length. The subjects shall be written and sealed by the chairman of the Program Committee and handed to the President before

the meeting begins. The speakers' names shall be drawn at random by the President from a list prepared by the Secretary. No member, however, shall be called upon to speak extemporaneously a second time during the year until every other member has been called upon once.

3. A *prepared debate* on some phase of the general topic. There shall be two speakers on each side, each speaker to have one constructive speech of not more than eight (8) minutes and one rebuttal speech of not more than four (4) minutes.

4. A *volunteeer debate* that shall follow the prepared debate and shall deal with the same question. It shall be open only to members who have not already appeared on the program. Each volunteer extemporaneous debater shall be limited to three (3) minutes and may speak not more than once.

5. *Judges' decision.* At the beginning of the prepared debate the President shall appoint three (3) judges who, after the volunteer debate shall give (a) a decision on the outcome of the prepared debate, and (b) a decision on the outcome of the volunteer debate. The two decisions shall be distinct and separate, and the one shall not influence the other. The judges shall not confer before writing their decisions. There shall be no appeal from their decisions.

Sect. C—*Special Programs*

From time to time on dates to be determined by the Club there may be special programs with invited speakers.

Article VI—Order of Business

In all regular meetings of the Club the order of exercises shall be as follows:

Part A—Program

1. Call to order.
2. Roll-call.
3. Program of speeches.

---

4. Recess of 5 minutes.

Part B—Business

5. Call to order.
6. Roll-call.
7. Reports of Critics.
8. Reading of the Minutes of the last previous meeting, and their approval.

9. Reports of Standing Committees and Boards.
    a. Membership Committee.
    b. Program Committee.
    c. Board of Censors.
10. Reports of Special Committees.
11. Special Orders.
12. Unfinished Business and General Orders.
13. New Business.
14. Adjournment.

Article VII—Suspension, Trial, and Expulsion of Members

Sect. A—*Causes of Suspension*

Not only shall a member be suspended for non-payment of dues and fines, as provided in Article I, Sect. B, and Article III, Sect. C of these Bylaws, but also, if he is found guilty of any misconduct that, in the judgment of the Club, is a detriment or discredit to the Club and its members, he may be deprived of membership.

Sect. B—*Arraignment*

A member who is thus charged with serious misconduct shall, upon authorization of the Club, be given written notice of the charges and shall be required to stand trial before the Club at its next regular business meeting. The defendant shall be allowed to choose counsel from the Club. Club members may be examined as witnesses. The order of procedure shall be as follows:

1. The President reads the charges and calls upon the defendant to reply.
2. The defendant, personally or through counsel, enters a plea. If he pleads "guilty," the Club, by a ⅔ vote, will pass sentence at once. If he pleads "not guilty," the trial will proceed as follows:
3. Witnesses are called and examined.
4. The defendant, either personally or through counsel, makes his defense and retires from the room.
5. The Club deliberates upon the question.
6. The President sums up the evidence and the arguments made.
7. The Club, voting by ballot, decides by a ⅔ vote the guilt or innocence of the defendant and, if the defendant is convicted, fixes the penalty.

There shall be no appeal from a verdict thus reached. A person thus convicted shall never be eligible for reinstatement.

Sect. C—*Appeals*

A person who has been suspended for non-payment of dues or fines may file a written appeal to the Club for a trial at any time during suspension and prior to his removal from membership, provided that the appeal is signed by five (5) members in good standing. The procedure in such a trial will be the same as that set forth above in Sect. B. No person shall have the right of appeal after his removal from membership, nor shall he be granted a second trial on the same charges.

Sect. D—*Rights of Suspended Members*

A person who has been suspended shall, during the period of his suspension, have none of the rights of members in good standing except—

1. The right to appeal his case to the Club and
2. The right to speak in his own defense at the trial.

Sect. E—*Reinstatement*

A member who has been suspended for non-payment of dues or fines may, at any time prior to his expulsion, apply for reinstatement and, if the causes of suspension have been removed, may be reinstated to membership by a ⅔ vote at any regular business meeting.

Article VIII—Amendments

Amendments to these Bylaws may be adopted at any regular business meeting of the Club by a majority vote, provided that written or printed notice of the proposed amendments has been given to all members at least one week previously.

Article IX—Parliamentary Authority

All questions of parliamentary procedure not covered by these Bylaws shall be decided according to the latest edition of *Funk & Wagnalls Book of Parliamentary Procedure* (Bridge).

E. Standing Rules—Basic Principles

Regulations that deal with the details of business procedure and that are adopted from time to time as they are needed are called Standing Rules. They may be adopted at any business meeting by a majority vote and without previous notice. Only a majority vote is needed to suspend them. If previous notice has been given, they may be amended or rescinded by a majority vote. If, however, previous notice has not been given, a ⅔ vote is necessary to amend or rescind them. No Standing Rule may be adopted if it conflicts with another rule previously adopted or with the Constitution or Bylaws.

F. Model Standing Rules

The following model rules will serve to illustrate the principles set forth above in Sect. E:

STANDING RULES
of the
JEFFERSON FORENSIC CLUB

1. Program meetings shall start at 7:30 P.M.
2. The Secretary shall call the roll twice at each meeting. On the second roll-call, which shall immediately follow the first, he shall call only the names of those who did not answer the first call.
3. At each program meeting there shall be two ushers appointed by the President.
4. While a meeting is in progress, no member shall cross the floor or leave the hall without permission of the President.
5. The President or a custodian appointed by him shall see that the hall is in good condition before the time of meeting. He shall have authority to employ a janitor for a wage approved by the Club.
6. As soon as judges have been appointed for a debate, the President shall order the Sergeant-at-Arms to deliver to each of them a blank ballot like the following model:

JUDGE'S BALLOT
In my opinion and without regard to the merits of the question, the more effective debating has been done by the _____side in the *prepared debate*
and the
_____side in the *volunteer debate*.
Signed: _____

---

7. After the Minutes have been corrected and approved, the Secretary shall make two (2) typewritten copies. One he shall deliver to the President; the other he himself shall keep in a looseleaf binder.
8. At the last meeting preceding the election of officers, i.e., at the first meeting in September and the first meeting in February, the President and two members appointed by him shall examine the Secretary's book and report on its condition before the order be given for transscribing the Minutes in the permanent record.
9. The Club shall provide three (3) keys to the hall: one for the President, one for the Secretary, and one for the custodian of the hall (Cf. Standing Rule No. 5). The Secretary and the custodian shall receive their keys from the President and at the end of their terms of service shall return the keys to him. The President, when he retires from office, shall deliver the keys to his successor.

10. Fines to be assessed against members (see Bylaws, Art. III, Sect. C) shall be as follows:

a. For absence from roll call . . . . $ .50
b. For non-performance of duty in office 1.00
c. For failure to appear on program when assigned . . . 1.00
d. For disorderly conduct in a meeting of the Club . . . 1.00
e. For frivolous or dilatory parliamentary tactics 50
f. For indecorum in debate 50

G. Index to Constitution, Bylaws, and Standing Rules

In connection with the constitution, bylaws, and standing rules of an organization there should be a comprehensive index listing all subjects alphabetically and giving the numbers of all pages on which there is pertinent information. The following model will serve as an illustration:

Index of the Constitution, Bylaws, and Standing Rules
of the
JEFFERSON FORENSIC CLUB [1]

[1] Pages 102–113.

NOTE

A society should provide each of its members with a printed or mimeographed copy of its Constitution, Bylaws, and Standing Rules. At the end of such a booklet may be left a few blank pages for recording amendments that are made from time to time, especially to the Standing Rules, which are more frequently changed than the Bylaws or the Constitution. Here may be entered also official interpretations of certain regulations and possibly some memoranda concerning desirable changes in the rules. The names of committee members could be listed, and data concerning conventions and other meetings might be recorded here.

CHAPTER XXI

LEGAL RIGHTS AND OBLIGATIONS

(Cf. *Corpus Juris Secundum,* published by the American Law Book Company, 272 Flatbush Ave. Extension, Brooklyn, N. Y.)

A. Legal Rights and Obligations of Societies

1. The Constitution and Bylaws of an organization are binding upon a member only if they were agreed to by him. If amendments were added later, however, a member who opposed the amendments is bound by them, as implied by his desire to continue his membership. If he does not wish to be bound by amendments to which he was and is opposed, he should resign.

2. A society is not bound by the acts of *members unauthorized* to perform them or by *unauthorized acts* of its duly appointed or elected representatives.

3. Dues, fines, and assessments levied by a society may, when overdue, be collected by legal action if they are personal obligations. Otherwise the society must depend upon its own rules for a remedy. Termination of membership by resignation or expulsion does not affect an obligation already incurred.

4. If an unincorporated society that is not operated for profit should contract a debt as a result of some transaction that is not within the proper scope of its avowed purposes and activities, the liability rests only on those members who, by expressed vote or implied consent, approved the transaction when it was proposed, or when it was in progress, or who later ratified it.

5. A society has the right to override a decision taken by its Board of Managers, except in cases where the Board has acted on authority expressly conferred upon it by the society.

6. A society is under obligation to give adequate previous notice to all its members when a special meeting is to be called. Such notice must tell the time, the place, and the purpose of the meeting, and in such a meeting no business may be transacted other than that named in the notice.

7. A society has the right to make and enforce its own rules and to impose penalties for breaking the rules, but in so doing it must not violate any state or federal law. It may suspend or expel a member in accordance with its own rules, which were subscribed to by the offending member, or, in general, for his violation of duty as a member or as a citizen, whether the rules so provide or not. In taking such action, however, it must proceed in the following manner, even when the rules of the society do not so provide:

   a. Give the member previous notice that action will be taken against him;
   b. Inform him of the charges against him;
   c. Allow him a reasonable time to prepare a defense; and
   d. Give him a trial, or the privilege of a trial, before an impartial tribunal. If the society should consider it necessary for its own protection to publish the fact that the offender's membership has been terminated, the greatest caution should be exercised in order to avoid making any statement that might be construed as libelous.

8. If an unincorporated society has illegally suspended or expelled a member, it or its members may be liable to the suspended or expelled person for damages resulting from—

   a. Depriving him of the use of the society's facilities;
   b. His unemployment due to the society's action; and
   c. His mental suffering due to his suspension or expulsion.

   Such liability will not be affected by reinstatement of the person.

9. A society may eject from its meeting any person who has no lawful right to be present, but, in doing so, it may use only reasonable force. Unduly harsh or abusive treatment of the intruder might be a tort resulting in action against the individual member who used unnecessary violence, but there would be no liability on the part of the society as a whole or on the part of the chairman who ordered the ejection.

10. If a local society is not independent but is a part of a larger organization by which it is controlled and governed, then, in case of a conflict between the two, a court will recognize the judgments of the larger organization as final and binding in all matters over which the local organization has jurisdiction. A civil court will not overrule a decision of a church organization on internal questions—such as matters of church custom, ecclesiastical law, discipline of members, or tenets of a faith—but, if a dispute on such matters is appealed to the court, will uphold the ruling of the highest church

authority or tribunal by which the case has been tried. If, on the other hand, a dispute involves the ownership of property, the civil court will exercise jurisdiction.

B. Legal Rights and Obligations of Members of a Society

1. If an organization is unincorporated, each member is personally liable for all debts and financial obligations incurred by the organization during the period of his membership. If his membership should be terminated, he would still be liable unless due notice had been given to the creditors. If the society is incorporated, however, the organization as a whole is responsible, and individual members are not personally liable.

2. In joining an organization a person agrees to certain specific rules and provisions of the society, usually signing his name to a promise that he will abide by these. Thus he enters into a binding legal contract.

3. If a member performs an unauthorized act tending to involve the society, he alone is responsible and liable. The society, of course, may assume the responsibility by ratifying or approving the act.

4. A member is legally responsible for dues, fines, and assessments if these are personal obligations to the society. Otherwise, he is not legally liable.

5. A member has no liability for dues or assessments levied before he joined the society or after he resigned from it. However, even after his resignation or expulsion, he is still liable for dues and assessments that were in default when his membership was terminated.

6. A suspended member of an organization is still considered a member and is liable, therefore, for dues and assessments pending his reinstatement or expulsion.

7. If an unincorporated society that is not operated for profit should contract a debt as a result of a transaction that is not within the scope of its purpose or activities, a member who did not approve or give his assent in any way when the transaction was proposed or when it was in progress and who did not later ratify the act, is not legally liable. A commercial organization, however, or any association for profit is regarded legally as a partnership, in which all members are individually liable for debts incurred by other members in the name of the organization.

8. Officers of a society are legally liable to their associates and to the society for fraud or for the mismanagement of funds intrusted to

them or for abuse of the society's facilities and resources for personal profit.

9. All members, even those who are delinquent in the payment of dues and other obligations or are suspended, have the right to vote at the election of officers, unless the regulations of the society stipulate otherwise.

10. If certain members try to violate the agreement of a society or to elect an officer illegally, their associates may bring suit to prevent such action.

11. No member of a society has the right to inspect the Minutes of its Board of Directors unless, by order of the society, the Minutes are made accessible to all members.

12. Every member of a society has the right to previous notice of special meetings and is entitled to know the time, place, and purpose of such meetings, whether the rules of the society provide for such notice or not.

13. A member of a society may be expelled for violation of the rules of the society, to which he has previously given assent; and, in general, for violation of his duty as a member or as a citizen, whether the rules so stipulate or not, provided that in the act of expulsion no state or federal law is violated; and provided, further, that the following steps have been taken, even when the rules of the society do not so provide:
    a. He has received previous notice that action would be taken against him;
    b. He has been informed of the charges against him;
    c. He has been given reasonable time to prepare a defense; and
    d. He has had a fair trial, or the privilege of a fair trial, before an impartial tribunal.

14. If a person is expelled from a society and the fact is published with an explanation containing malicious misrepresentations or defamatory comments concerning him, he may enter an action for libel against the society.

15. A person who has been illegally suspended or expelled from an unincorporated society may bring suit against the society or its members for damages resulting to him from—
    a. Being deprived of the use of the facilities of the society;
    b. Unemployment due to his suspension or expulsion; and
    c. Mental suffering due to his suspension or expulsion.
His claims will not be impaired by his reinstatement.

Chapter XXII

ARRAIGNMENT AND TRIAL

A. Causes

Any member of a society may be suspended or expelled for reasons set forth in the Bylaws, which have been subscribed to by him; for immoral conduct or any serious misbehavior that, in the judgment of the society, is a discredit or detriment to the society and its members; or, in general, for any violation of his duty as a member or as a citizen.

B. Procedure

If a member is brought to trial, the procedure is generally as follows:

1. The charges are investigated, usually by a committee.
2. The committee reports its findings to the society and makes a recommendation.
3. If suspension or expulsion is recommended, a date is set for an adjourned meeting.
4. The offending member is informed of the charge against him and is summoned to appear at the adjourned meeting to stand trial. He must be given adequate time to prepare a defense.
5. When the trial is called, the report of the investigating committee, if there is one, is presented.
6. The defendant, personally or through counsel, enters a plea. If he pleads "guilty," the society, by a ⅔ vote, passes sentence at once. If he pleads "not guilty," the trial continues as follows:
    a. Witnesses for the society are called and examined.
    b. Witnesses for the defendant are called and examined.
    c. Rebuttal testimony is presented.
    d. Witnesses may be cross-examined.
    e. The defendant, either personally or through counsel, makes his defense and retires from the room.
    f. The society debates the question.
    g. The President sums up the evidence and the arguments and then puts the question to a vote.

120

h. The society, voting by ballot, decides by a ⅔ vote the innocence or guilt of the defendant and, if he is found guilty,
fixes the penalty.

i. The defendant is informed of the outcome of the trial.

CHAPTER XXIII

MODEL BUSINESS MEETINGS

First Model Meeting
MAIN MOTIONS

PRESIDENT: *(Tapping table with gavel.)* The meeting will come to order. The Secretary will call the roll.

Call to order

SECRETARY: *(Sitting at desk, reads the roll of members. At the conclusion of the roll-call he rereads the names of those who did not answer.)*

Roll-call

PRESIDENT: The Secretary will read the minutes of the last meeting.

Reading of Minutes

SECRETARY: *(Rising.)* Mr. President . . . . *(Reads the Minutes.)*

PRESIDENT: Are there any corrections or additions to the Minutes?

MR. A: MR. President.

PRESIDENT: MR. A.

MR. A: The report states that the annual meeting is to be held on Saturday, March 10. I call attention to the fact that the 10th is Friday instead of Saturday. The date set for the meeting is March 11.

Correcting the Minutes

PRESIDENT: The Secretary will please correct the error. Are there any further corrections or any additions?

MR. B: MR. President.

PRESIDENT: MR. B.

MR. B: The Minutes show that the Chair was to appoint a committee to make preparation for the annual meeting, but the Minutes do not state who the members of the committee are. Should not their names be recorded in the Minutes?

PRESIDENT:	They should. The omission was an oversight. The members of the committee are MR. A, MR. B, and MR. C, MR. A being the chairman. The secretary will please see that these names are entered in the proper place in the Minutes. Are there any further corrections or additions? (*Pause.*) If not, the Minutes are approved as read and corrected. We shall now have the report of the treasurer, MR. D.	*Further corrections*
		Approved by general consent
TREASURER:	(*Rising*) MR. President. (*Reads his report.*)	
PRESIDENT:	What shall be done with this report?	
MR. E:	MR. President.	
PRESIDENT:	MR. E.	
MR. E:	I move that the report be accepted.	*To accept a report*
MR. F:	(*Seated*) I second the motion.	
PRESIDENT:	It is moved by MR. E and seconded by MR. F that the report be accepted. Is there any discussion? (*Discussion follows, in which questions are asked and answered and comments are made on the report.*)	
MR. G:	MR. President.	
PRESIDENT:	MR. G.	
MR. G:	Has the report been audited as required by our Bylaws?	
PRESIDENT:	Yes. The auditor's report has been filed with the secretary. Will the secretary please read the report of the auditor?	*Auditor's report*
SECRETARY:	MR. President, the report is as follows: (*Reads the report.*)	
PRESIDENT:	You have heard the statement of the auditor that the treasurer's report is correct. Are you ready for the question?	
SEVERAL:	(*Seated*) Question.	
PRESIDENT:	The question is on MR. E's motion to accept the treasurer's report. All those in favor will say "aye." (*They vote.*) All those opposed will say "no." (*They vote.*) The motion is carried. (*The treasurer delivers a copy of his report to the secretary for recording.*) We shall next proceed to the reports of standing committees. First we shall hear from the Legislative Committee.	*Report delivered to secretary for filing*

MR. H:	(*Rising*) MR. President.
PRESIDENT:	MR. H.
MR. H:	The Legislative Committee submits the following report: (*reads the report*).
PRESIDENT:	What shall be done with this report?
MR. J:	MR. President.
PRESIDENT:	MR. J.
MR. J:	I move that the report be adopted.
MR. K:	(*Seated*) I second the motion.
PRESIDENT:	You have heard the motion. Is there any discussion?
	(*Discussion. Vote is taken as in the case of the treasurer's report above.*)
	The motion is carried. Next will be the report of the Publicity Committee.
	(*This report and others that follow are handled in the manner illustrated above. After the reports of standing committees have all been disposed of—*)
	We pass now to the reports of special committees. Does the Committee on Convention Arrangements have a report to make at this time?
MR. L:	(*Chairman of Committee on Convention Arrangements*) MR. President.
PRESIDENT:	MR. L.
MR. L:	The committee has had two meetings thus far and desires to report as follows: (*Reads his report*).
PRESIDENT:	You have heard the report of the committee on arrangements. What shall be done with it?
	(*This report and the reports of other special committees are disposed of in the manner illustrated above.*)
	The reports of special committees having been finished, we pass to the head of Unfinished Business. Is there any unfinished business to come before the meeting today?
MR. M:	MR. President.
PRESIDENT:	MR. M.
MR. M:	At the last preceding meeting and also at

Reports of standing committees

To adopt a report

Reports of special committees

Unfinished business

	meetings prior to that we discussed the question of refinancing the mortgage on our club property. (*After a discussion of the financial problem, he concludes by saying—*) Therefore I move that the treasurer and the directors be instructed and empowered to take the necessary steps to refinance the mortgage at the lowest possible rate.
MR. N:	(*Seated*) I second the motion.
PRESIDENT:	You have heard the motion. Is there any discussion? (*Discussion follows, at the conclusion of which the Chair says—*) Are you ready for the question?
SEVERAL:	(*Seated*) Question.
PRESIDENT:	All those in favor of the motion will say "aye." (*They vote.*) Those opposed will say "no." (*They vote.*) The motion is carried. Is there any other unfinished business? (*Other business is brought up and disposed of in a similar manner. When unfinished business has all been disposed of, the Chair says—*) The next order of business is New Business. What new business should come before this meeting? (*New business, if there is any, is presented and dealt with in the manner just illustrated. At the conclusion of New Business, the Chair says—*) If there is no further business, the Chair will entertain a motion to adjourn.
MR. Q:	MR. President.
PRESIDENT:	MR. Q.
MR. Q:	I move that the meeting be now adjourned.
PRESIDENT:	You have heard the motion to adjourn. Is there a second?
MR. R:	(*Seated*) I second the motion.
PRESIDENT:	The motion has been seconded. All those in favor will say "aye." (*They vote.*) All those opposed will say "no." (*They vote.*) The motion is carried, and the meeting is adjourned. (*Taps the desk with the gavel and leaves the chair.*)

New business

*"To adjourn"
unqualified*

Second Model Meeting
SUBSIDIARY MOTIONS

	(*The first part of the meeting is omitted here.*)	
PRESIDENT:	Is there any new business to be presented at this meeting?	*New business*
MR. R:	MR. President.	
PRESIDENT:	MR. R.	
MR. R:	It seems to me that in the past our club has been inadequately represented at the annual convention. (*He gives reasons.*) Therefore I move that our usual appropriation for delegates be increased this year by $150 in order to send an additional delegate to the national convention in New York City.	
MR. S:	(*Seated*) I second the motion.	
PRESIDENT:	You have heard the motion. Is there any discussion?	
MR. T:	MR. President.	
PRESIDENT:	MR. T.	
MR. T:	I favor the motion in general, but the usual amount of $150 per delegate may be insufficient this year. It may be necessary later to vote a larger appropriation than usual for all delegates. Therefore I move to amend the motion by inserting the words "or more if necessary" after the figure $150.	*To amend*
MR. U:	(*Seated*) I second the motion.	
PRESIDENT:	You have heard the motion to amend. Do you want to discuss it?	
MR. V:	MR. President.	
PRESIDENT:	MR. V.	
MR. V:	There should be certain safeguards in an action of this kind. Therefore I move to amend the amendment by inserting the words "the club considers it" between the words "if" and "necessary," so that the amendment will read "if the club considers it necessary."	*To amend the proposed amendment*
PRESIDENT:	Is there a second? (*Pause.*)	
MR. W:	(*Seated*) I second the motion.	

PRESIDENT:	It is seconded by MR. W. You have heard MR. V's motion to amend the amendment. Is there any discussion?
MR. X:	MR. President.
PRESIDENT:	MR. X.
MR. X:	I am opposed to MR. R's motion providing for an extra appropriation for an additional delegate because . . .
PRESIDENT:	(*Interrupting*) MR. X is out of order. The question immediately pending is on MR. V's motion to amend the amendment.
MR. Y:	MR. President.
PRESIDENT:	MR. Y.
MR. Y:	I should like to propose a more satisfactory phrase to substitute for MR. V's expression. Therefore I move . . .
PRESIDENT:	(*Interrupting*) The gentleman is out of order. An amendment to an amendment cannot be amended.
MR. A:	MR. President.
PRESIDENT:	MR. A.
MR. A:	I move to refer MR. R's motion to a committee of three members to be appointed by the Chair.
MR. B:	(*Seated*) I second the motion.
PRESIDENT:	You have heard the motion to commit. Is there any discussion?
MR. C:	MR. President.
PRESIDENT:	MR. C.
MR. C:	I do not believe that a committee could decide the matter any better than the club could if it had a little time to think it over. I move that MR. R's motion be postponed until our next regular meeting.
MR. D:	(*Seated*) I second the motion.
PRESIDENT:	It has been moved by MR. C and seconded by MR. D that action on MR. R's original motion be postponed to our next regular meeting. Is there any debate on this question?
MR. E:	MR. President.

"Out of order"

"Out of order"

To commit

To postpone to a definite time

PRESIDENT:	MR. E.
MR. E:	I move to postpone it indefinitely.
PRESIDENT:	The motion is out of order. A motion to postpone to a definite time takes precedence over a motion to postpone indefinitely.

"Out of order"

MR. F: ⎱	
MR. G: ⎬	MR. President.
MR. H: ⎰	
PRESIDENT:	The Chair recognizes MR. F.
MR. F:	I move to lay MR. R's original motion on the table.

To lay on the table

MR. G:	(*Seated*) I second the motion.
MR. H:	MR. President.
PRESIDENT:	To what question does the gentleman rise?
MR. H:	I am opposed to this motion because . . .
PRESIDENT:	(*Interrupting*) The gentleman is out of order. A motion "to lay on the table" is not debatable. All those in favor of the motion to table MR. R's motion will say "aye." (*They vote.*) Those opposed will say "no." (*They vote.*) The motion is lost. The question now is on MR. C's motion to postpone action on MR. R's motion until our next regular meeting. Is there any further discussion of that motion?

"Out of order"

MR. J:	MR. President.
PRESIDENT:	MR. J.
MR. J:	I move that debate on the motion to postpone be closed.

To close debate

MR. K:	(*Seated*) I second the motion.
MR. L:	MR. President.
PRESIDENT:	To what question does the gentleman rise?
MR. L:	I do not think that debate should be closed because . . .
PRESIDENT:	(*Interrupting*) The gentleman is out of order. A motion "to close debate" is not debatable. The Chair reminds the club that a ⅔ vote is required to pass the motion "to close debate." All those in favor of the motion will please stand. (*They vote and are counted by the secretary.*) Those opposed will now

"Out of order"

A ⅔ majority needed

stand. (*They vote and are counted.*) The motion is carried.

The question now is on MR. C's motion to postpone. All those in favor of that motion will say "aye." (*They vote.*) All those opposed will say "no." (*They vote.*) The motion is lost.

The question now is on MR. A's motion to refer MR. R's motion to a committee of three to be appointed by the Chair. Is there any further discussion of MR. A's motion? (*Pause.*) Are you ready for the question?

SEVERAL: Question.

PRESIDENT: The question has been called for. All those in favor will say "aye." (*They vote.*) All those opposed will say "no." (*They vote.*) The motion is lost.

Motions disposed of in order of precedence

The question now is on MR. V's motion to amend the amendment. Is there any further debate of that motion? (*Pause.*) If not, all those in favor will say "aye." (*They vote.*) Those opposed will say "no." (*They vote.*) The motion is carried.

The question now is on MR. T's amendment as amended. The Secretary will read his motion with the amendment just adopted.

SECRETARY: MR. President, MR. T's amendment was as follows: . . . . . . It was amended to read . . . .

PRESIDENT: Is there any further discussion? (*Pause.*) If not, all those in favor will say "aye." (*They vote.*) Those opposed will say "no." (*They vote.*) The motion is carried.

The question now is on MR. R's original motion as amended. The Secretary will please read the motion as modified by amendments just passed.

SECRETARY: MR. President, MR. R's motion as amended is as follows: . . . .

PRESIDENT: Do you wish to debate this motion any further?

MR. M: MR. President.

PRESIDENT: MR. M.

MR. M: I am of the opinion . . . . (*he argues for or against the motion*).
              (*Others follow until much time has been spent.*)

MR. N: MR. President.

PRESIDENT: MR. N.

MR. N: I think that the question has been debated long enough. Everyone has had a chance to express his opinion. Therefore I move that the Previous Question be ordered.

SEVERAL: I second the motion.

PRESIDENT: The motion is seconded by MR. O. All those in favor will say "aye." (*They vote.*) All opposed will say "no." (*They vote.*) There being a ⅔ majority in favor, the motion is carried, and the Previous Question is ordered; i.e., it is ordered that all debate be stopped and the vote be taken at once on the pending question, which is MR. R's original motion. All in favor of that motion will say "aye." (*They vote.*) All those opposed will say "no." (*They vote.*) There being a majority of votes in favor, the motion is carried. An appropriation for an additional delegate this year will be made accordingly.
              Is there any further business that should come before this meeting?

MR. P: MR. President.

PRESIDENT: MR. P.

MR. P: I move that we take a recess of one hour.

MR. Q: (*Seated*) I second the motion.

PRESIDENT: It has been moved and seconded that we take a recess of one hour. Is there any discussion? (*Pause.*) If not, are you ready for the question?

SEVERAL: Question.

PRESIDENT: The question has been called for. All those in favor will say "aye." (*They vote.*) Those opposed will say "no." (*They vote.*) The mo-

"Previous question" is ordered

Vote on original main motion as amended

To take a recess

tion is carried. There will be a recess of one
hour, and this session will be resumed at —
o'clock. (*He taps the table with the gavel
and leaves the chair.*)

(*The remainder of the meeting is omitted here.*)

Third Model Meeting
INCIDENTAL MOTIONS

(*First part of meeting is omitted here.*)

PRESIDENT:	We shall now pass to the head of New Business. Is there any new business that should be brought before this meeting?	*New business*
MR. A:	MR. President.	
PRESIDENT:	MR. A.	
MR. A:	I wish to offer the following resolution: "Whereas this club has long followed a policy of racial discrimination in admitting persons to membership, and	*Offering a resolution*

"Whereas this policy has been detrimental to
our best interests (*etc.*), therefore

"Be it resolved that hereafter it shall be our
policy to admit persons regardless of race."
I move the adoption of this resolution. (*He
delivers a copy to the secretary.*)

MR. B:	I second the motion.	
MR. C:	MR. President.	
MR. D:	MR. President.	
MR. E:	MR. President, I object to the consideration of the question.	*Objection to consideration*
PRESIDENT:	Consideration of the question has been objected to. Shall the question be considered? All those in favor will please stand. (*They vote and are counted.*)	

Please be seated. All those opposed will now
stand. (*They vote and are counted.*)

Since there is not a ⅔ majority opposed to
consideration, the objection is not sustained.
The motion will be considered.   *A ⅔ vote
needed*

MR. C:	MR. President, I rise to a question of information.	*Request for information*
PRESIDENT:	The member will state his question.	
MR. C:	Does the Constitution of the club contain any restrictions as to racial qualifications of prospective members?	
PRESIDENT:	The Chair believes that it does not.	
MR. D:	MR. President, I rise to a parliamentary inquiry.	*Parliamentary inquiry*
PRESIDENT:	The member will state his inquiry.	
MR. D:	Is it not true that the passing of this resolution would be equivalent to amending the Constitution and, since the Constitution can be amended only after previous notice, it would be unparliamentary to consider and vote upon this resolution until the next meeting of the club?	
PRESIDENT:	The Chair is of the opinion that such is not the case, but that the resolution, if adopted, would operate as a Standing Rule. Is there any further discussion of the motion to adopt the resolution?	
MR. E:	MR. President, I rise to a point of order.	*Point of order*
PRESIDENT:	The member will state his point.	
MR. E:	The parliamentary point raised by MR. D a moment ago is well taken, it seems to me, and this motion "to adopt" is out of order.	
PRESIDENT:	The Chair rules that the motion is in order.	
MR. E:	MR. President, I appeal from the decision of the Chair.	*Appeal*
PRESIDENT:	Is there a second to this appeal?	
MR. F:	I second it.	
PRESIDENT:	An appeal has been made by MR. E and seconded by MR. F. Do you wish to debate it? (*A long discussion follows. Finally—*)	*Table, A, col. (e)*
MR. G:	MR. President.	
PRESIDENT:	MR. G.	
MR. G:	I call for the Previous Question on the appeal.	*"Previous question" on an appeal*
MR. H:	I second the call.	
PRESIDENT:	All those in favor of ordering the Previous Question on the appeal will say "aye." (*They*	

vote.) All who are opposed will say "no." (*They vote*.) The motion is carried, and the Previous Question has been ordered. Therefore the appeal will be put to a vote. The question before the club now is: Does the club sustain the Chair in his decision that the motion to adopt the resolution is in order? All who are in favor will say "aye." (*They vote*.) All who are opposed will say "no." (*They vote*.) The motion is carried, and the decision of the Chair stands as the decision of the club.

The question now is on MR. A's motion to adopt the resolution that he presented. Is there any further discussion?

MR. A:	MR. President.
PRESIDENT:	MR. A.
MR. A:	I did not anticipate that my resolution would cause such agitation in the club. Perhaps it was unwise. I therefore request permission to withdraw my motion.

Permission to withdraw a resolution

PRESIDENT:	Does the second give his consent?
MR. B:	(*Seated*) I consent.
PRESIDENT:	If there is no objection, the request is granted. (*The Chair waits, but hears no objection*.) Is there any further new business to be presented at this session?

General consent

MR. G:	MR. President.
PRESIDENT:	MR. G.
MR. G:	The membership of our club has been growing gradually smaller for several years, so that today we have scarcely enough members to carry out our program effectively. Therefore I move that we immediately start a drive for 200 new members.
MR. H:	I second the motion.
PRESIDENT:	You have heard the motion. Is there any discussion? (*Discussion follows*.)
MR. J:	MR. President.
PRESIDENT:	MR. J.

MR. J:	I favor the motion in general, but I consider the number 200 to be much too large. I therefore move to amend the motion by striking out the figure 200 and substituting the figure 100.	*To amend a main motion*
MR. K:	I second the motion.	
PRESIDENT:	You have heard the motion to amend. Is there any discussion of it?	
MR. L:	I agree with MR. J that 200 members would be too many, but 100 would be too few. (*He gives his reasons.*) Therefore I move to amend the amendment by striking out the figure 100 and substituting the figure 150.	*To amend the proposed amendment*
MR. M:	I second the motion.	
PRESIDENT:	You have heard MR. L's motion to amend the amendment. Do you wish to discuss it?	
MR. N:	MR. President.	
PRESIDENT:	MR. N.	
MR. N:	I believe that even 100 new members are more than we actually need in order to operate efficiently. I should favor 50 as an adequate number.	
PRESIDENT:	Since there are several numbers to be voted on, ranging from 200 down to 50, if there is no objection, the motion will be treated as having a blank for the number. (*He waits for an objection, but none is made.*) In the first place, does any member favor a number larger than 200?	*Creating a blank* *General consent*
MR. P:	MR. President.	
PRESIDENT:	MR. P.	
MR. P:	I believe that 250 or even 300 would not be too large a number.	
PRESIDENT:	Are there any other suggestions? (*He waits.*) The Chair, then, will ask for a vote on each number, starting with the highest. All those who favor the number 300 will please rise. (*They vote and are counted by the secretary.*) Since there is not a majority for this number, all those in favor of the number 250 will please rise. (*They vote and are count-*	*Voting on largest number first*

ed.) This number also did not receive a majority. Those in favor of the number 200 will please rise. (*They vote and are counted.*) There is no majority yet. The next number suggested was 150. As many as favor this number will please stand. (*They vote and are counted.*) The count is. . . , which is a majority of . . . , the number of members present. The number 150, then, is the number that will be inserted in the blank. The question now is on the amended motion, which reads as follows: "that we immediately start a drive for 150 new members." Do you wish to discuss it further?

Division of assembly in voting

SEVERAL: Question.

PRESIDENT: The question is called for. All those in favor of the motion as amended will say "aye." (*They vote.*) Those not in favor will say "no." (*They vote.*) The Chair believes that the motion is carried.

MR. N: (*Rising*) I call for a division of the club.

A division is demanded

PRESIDENT: A division is called for; therefore the vote will be taken again. All those in favor of the motion will stand and be counted. (*They vote.*) Those opposed will now stand. (*They vote.*) The count is . . . in favor and . . . against. The motion is carried by a majority of . . . Is there any further new business to be brought up at this time?

MR. R: Mr. President.

PRESIDENT: MR. R.

MR. R: Our members, as everyone is aware, come from a wide area. It has been the custom of the club to remind all members of the date of each meeting and to send the notice by mail a few days before the meeting. This practice does very well for those within a distance of ten miles of the meeting place, but those who come from greater distances often do not get their notices in sufficient time. Therefore I move that the members living at a distance exceeding ten miles be notified by telegram and that the cost of the telegram be deducted from the traveling expense allowance permitted by our Bylaws.

MR. S: I second the motion.

PRESIDENT: You have heard the motion. Do you wish to discuss it?

MR. T: MR. President.

PRESIDENT: MR. T.

MR. T: This motion is really two motions; therefore I move that we divide the question and discuss first the part dealing with sending notices by telegram. *To divide the question*

MR. B: I second the motion.

PRESIDENT: All in favor will say "aye." (*They vote.*) Those opposed will say "no." (*They vote.*) The motion is carried. The question first is on the motion to send notices by telegram to those living farther than ten miles away. Is there any debate on this question? (*Discussion follows. Finally—*)

Are you ready for the question?

MR. H: Question.

PRESIDENT: (*After waiting to be sure that no one else wishes to speak.*) All those in favor of the motion will say "aye." (*They vote.*) Those opposed will say "no." (*They vote.*) The motion is carried.

The question now is on the second part of the motion, which proposes that the cost of the telegram be deducted from the allowance for traveling expense. Do you wish to discuss it? (*Discussion follows. When it lags and no one any longer seeks the floor, the president says—*)

If there is no further discussion, the question will be put. (*Pause.*) All those in favor of the motion will say "aye." (*They vote overwhelmingly in favor.*) The motion is carried. *The Chair makes an error*

MR. V: MR. President, I rise to a point of order.

PRESIDENT: The member will state his point.

MR. V:	The Chair did not take the negative vote.	*Point of order*
PRESIDENT:	The point is well taken. The omission was unintentional. The Chair apologizes. All those who are opposed to the motion will say "no." (*They vote.*) The motion is carried, and, in accordance with the action just taken, the secretary hereafter will send notices by telegram to all members residing more than ten miles from here and will deliver a statement of the costs to the treasurer, who will deduct such costs from the traveling expenses refunded.	
	Is there any further business to be presented now?	
MR. W:	MR. President.	
PRESIDENT:	MR. W.	
MR. W:	I move that our next meeting be called an hour earlier than usual. (*He gives his reasons.*)	
MR. X:	I second the motion.	
PRESIDENT:	You have heard MR. W's motion. It amounts to a motion to suspend one of the Standing Rules of the club. Do you wish to discuss it?	*To suspend a standing rule*
SEVERAL:	Question.	
MR. Z:	MR. President, I rise to a question of privilege.	*A question of privilege*
PRESIDENT:	The member will state his question.	
MR. Z:	My presence is required immediately by the auditors, who are now checking accounts in the club office. I ask permission to leave the meeting.	
PRESIDENT:	If there is no objection, permission is granted. (MR. Z leaves.) The question before the club is on MR. W's motion that our next meeting be called an hour earlier than usual. All who are in favor will say "aye." (*They vote.*) All who are opposed will say "no." (*They vote.*) There being a majority in favor, the motion is carried.	*General consent*
		See p. 37, E
	Is there any further business that should be brought before the club at the present session?	

Mr. L:	Mr. President.
PRESIDENT:	Mr. L.
Mr. L:	As every member is aware, the Bylaws of the club, not having been revised in a very long time, now contain many defects and inconsistencies, etc. This matter has been brought to our attention on many occasions, but nothing has been done. I move, therefore, that a committee of five members be appointed by the Chair to revise the Bylaws and report at our next regular monthly meeting.
PRESIDENT:	Is there a second to this motion?
Mr. J:	I second the motion.
PRESIDENT:	It has been moved by Mr. L and seconded by Mr. J that— (*he repeats the motion*). Do you wish to discuss the motion? (*Discussion follows. Then, when it lags—*) Are you ready for the question?
SEVERAL:	Question.
PRESIDENT:	All those in favor of the motion will say "aye." (*They vote.*) Those opposed will say "no." (*They vote.*) There being a majority in favor, the motion is carried. Accordingly, the Chair appoints Mr. L, Mr. J, Mr E, Mr. H, and Mr. R as members of the committee. Mr. L will be the chairman. Is there any further business?
Mr. G:	Mr. President.
PRESIDENT:	Mr. G.
Mr. G:	Those who are familiar with the work in the club office know how inadequate our filing equipment is. (*He explains fully.*) Therefore I move that the club authorize the purchase of a new filing cabinet to meet the requirements of the office.
Mr. —:	I second the motion.
PRESIDENT:	Who seconded the motion?
Mr. M:	(*Raising his hand*) I seconded it. "M" is the name.
PRESIDENT:	It is moved by Mr. G and seconded by Mr.

To appoint a special committee

Chairman named first

	M that— (*he repeats the motion*). Is there any debate on this motion?
MR. R:	MR. President.
PRESIDENT:	MR. R.
MR. R:	I move to postpone the question indefinitely.
PRESIDENT:	Is there a second? (*He waits, but there is no response. Then—*) The motion is lost for want of a second.
MR. C:	MR. President.
PRESIDENT:	MR. C.
MR. C:	I move to amend the main motion of MR. G by adding the words "at a cost not to exceed $75."
MR. B:	I second the motion to amend.
PRESIDENT:	The question now is on MR. C's motion to amend. Is there any discussion of it?
MR. E:	MR. President.
PRESIDENT:	MR. E.
MR. E:	I move to amend the amendment by adding the words "unless approved by the Executive Committee."
MR. J:	I second the motion to amend the amendment.
PRESIDENT:	You have heard the motion. The question before you is on the motion to amend the amendment by adding the words "unless approved by the Executive Committee." Do you wish to discuss it?
MR. T:	MR. President.
PRESIDENT:	MR. T.
MR. T:	I move to refer MR. G's original motion to the Executive Committee.
MR. O:	I second the motion.
PRESIDENT:	You have heard the motion to commit. Will you discuss it? (*Discussion follows.*)
SEVERAL:	Question.
MR. P:	MR. President.
PRESIDENT:	MR. P.
MR. P:	I move to postpone the question until the next meeting.
MR. V:	I second MR. P's motion to postpone.

To amend the main motion

To amend an amendment

To commit

To postpone to a definite time

PRESIDENT:	Will you discuss the motion to postpone?	
MR. D:	MR. President.	
PRESIDENT:	MR. D.	
MR. D:	I move to amend MR. P's motion to postpone by adding the words "and that it be made a special order of business."	*To amend and make a special order*
PRESIDENT:	Is there a second?	
MR. F:	I second it.	
PRESIDENT:	You have heard the proposed amendment. A ⅔ majority is necessary for passage. Is there any discussion?	
MR. Q:	MR. President.	
PRESIDENT:	MR. Q.	
MR. Q:	I move the Previous Question on MR. G's original motion to authorize the purchase of a filing cabinet.	*"Previous question"*
MR. W:	I second the motion.	
MR. H:	MR. President, I rise to a parliamentary inquiry.	*Parliamentary inquiry*
PRESIDENT:	The member may state his inquiry.	
MR. H:	What will be the effect of the call for Previous Question, if passed?	
PRESIDENT:	If the Previous Question is ordered by a ⅔ vote, which is the required majority, the effect will be to stop all debate and force a vote at once on all pending motions.	
MR. I:	MR. President.	
PRESIDENT:	MR. I.	
MR. I:	I am opposed to stopping debate—	
PRESIDENT:	(*Interrupting*) The member is out of order. The call for Previous Question is not debatable. All in favor of ordering the Previous Question will stand. (*They stand and are counted.*) Those opposed will now stand. (*They stand and are counted.*) Since there is not a ⅔ majority in favor, the motion is lost.	*"Out of order"*
MR. H:	MR. President.	
PRESIDENT:	MR. H.	
MR. H:	I move a reconsideration of the vote on the Previous Question because I have discovered	

	that some did not understand the meaning of Previous Question and voted on the side which they did not favor.	
PRESIDENT:	On which side did MR. H vote?	
MR. H:	I voted in favor of the motion.	
PRESIDENT:	Then the member is out of order. A motion to reconsider may be made only by a person who voted on the prevailing side.	*"Out of order"*
MR. X:	MR. President.	
PRESIDENT:	MR. X.	
MR. X:	I voted on the prevailing side, and I move a reconsideration.	*To reconsider*
PRESIDENT:	MR. X's motion is in order. Is there a second?	
MR. A:	I second it.	
MR. J:	MR. President.	
PRESIDENT:	To what point does the member rise?	
MR. J:	I do not see any reason why the vote should be taken again, for—	
PRESIDENT:	(*Interrupting*) The member is out of order. A motion to reconsider is not debatable if the motion to which it applies is undebatable. In the present case it applies to Previous Question, which is always undebatable.	*"Out of order"*
	The question immediately pending is on the motion to reconsider. All who are in favor will say "aye." (*They vote.*) Those opposed will say "no." (*They vote.*) The motion is carried; therefore it will be necessary to take the vote again on the Previous Question. As many as are in favor of ordering the Previous Question will please stand. (*They stand and are counted.*) Those opposed will please stand. (*They stand and are counted.*) The motion is carried by a very large majority; consequently the Previous Question is ordered.	*Vote on motion "to reconsider"* *Vote on "Previous Question*
	The question now immediately pending is on MR. D's motion to amend MR. P's motion by adding the words "and that it be made a special order of business." A ⅔ ma-	

jority is required to make a special order of business. All in favor will stand. (*They stand and are counted.*) All opposed will stand. (*They stand and are counted.*) The count is . . . to . . . There being less than a ⅔ majority in favor, MR. D's motion is lost. *Vote on making a special order*

Motion lost for lack of ⅔ majority

The question now is on MR. P's motion to postpone the question of authorizing the purchase of a filing cabinet until the next meeting. All those in favor will say "aye." (*They vote.*) All those opposed will say "no." (*They vote.*) The motion is lost.

The question next is on the amendment to the amendment of the original motion; i.e., that the words be added, "unless approved by the Executive Committee." *Voting on motion to amend the proposed amendment yields to motion "to lay the original motion on the table"*

MR. Y:	MR. President.
PRESIDENT:	MR. Y.
MR. Y:	I move to lay MR. G's original motion on the table.
MR. N:	I second the motion.
MR. D:	MR. President.
PRESIDENT:	To what question does the member rise?
MR. D:	I move to amend the motion—
PRESIDENT:	(*Interrupting*) The member is out of order. No subsidiary motion can be applied to a motion to Lay on the Table. All those in favor of the motion to lay MR. G's original motion on the table will say "aye." (*They vote.*) All those opposed will say "no." (*They vote.*) There being a majority of votes in favor of the motion, it is carried.
MR. R:	MR. President, I rise to a point of order.
PRESIDENT:	The member may state the point.
MR. R:	There was not a ⅔ majority in favor. How, then, can the Chair declare the motion passed?
PRESIDENT:	Only an ordinary majority is required to pass a motion to Lay on the Table, except in meetings where the motion is habitually used to kill other motions. The Chair believes that

"Out of order"

Point of order

Cf. pp. 27–28

	the record will show that the motion is not so used in this club.	
MR. R:	MR. President, I appeal from the decision of the Chair.	*Appeal*
PRESIDENT:	Is there a second? (*He waits, but hears no second.*) The appeal is lost for want of a second.	
	Is there any other business that should be brought to the attention of the club at the present session? (*He waits a reasonable time, but no one rises to seek the floor. Therefore, tapping the desk with the gavel, he announces—*)	
	The meeting is adjourned until the . . . day of next month at . . . . o'clock, which is one hour earlier than the usual time. (*He lays down the gavel and leaves the desk.*)	*Chairman adjourns the meeting*

Fourth Model Meeting
AMENDING THE BYLAWS

	(*First part of meeting omitted here.*)	
PRESIDENT:	The next order of business is the reports of special committees. First we shall have the report of the committee appointed to revise the Bylaws. The Chair calls on MR. L, who is the chairman of that committee.	*Reports of special committees*
MR. L:	MR. President.	
PRESIDENT:	MR. L.	
MR. L:	The committee has mimeographed its report and has enough copies for all the members. May I have these distributed before the discussion starts?	*Mimeographed copies of proposed revision*
PRESIDENT:	Will MR. J and MR. E, who are members of the committee, please distribute copies of the report. (*The Chair waits. Then—*) Is there anyone now who did not get a copy of the report? If so, will you please raise your hand.	

	(*Everybody apparently is supplied.*) What procedure do you wish to follow in considering the report?	
MR. H:	MR. President.	
PRESIDENT:	MR. H.	
MR. H:	I move that we consider one article or one paragraph at a time.	*Seriatim*
MR. R:	I second the motion.	
PRESIDENT:	Do you wish to discuss this motion? (*Pause.*) If not, are you ready for the question?	
SEVERAL:	Question.	
PRESIDENT:	All who are in favor of the motion will say "aye." (*They vote.*) All those opposed will say "no." (*They vote.*) The motion is carried. Will MR. L please read the first article or paragraph.	
MR. L:	Article I, concerning . . . . Sect. 1 (*He reads.*) Sect. 2 (*He reads.*) (*Etc.*)	
PRESIDENT:	Does the club wish to discuss Article I? (*Discussion follows, in which amendments are proposed and adopted or rejected, but there should be no motion to adopt an article or paragraph.*) If there is no further discussion, the next article will be read.	
MR. L:	(*Reads Article II, section by section as before, giving explanations where needed.*)	
PRESIDENT:	Do you wish to discuss Article II? (*Discussion follows as before. Amendments are proposed and adopted or rejected. All speakers must address the Chair and be recognized. Their questions are referred by the Chair to MR. L.*) If there is no further discussion of this article, we shall examine the next article.	*Proposed amendments to Bylaws are treated as main motions*
MR. L:	Article III, concerning . . . . (*The procedure indicated above is repeated here.*)	
PRESIDENT:	(*Conducts the discussion as indicated above.*) If there is no further discussion, we shall pass to Article IV.	

MR. L: We propose no change in Article IV. We
                    believe that it is satisfactory as it stands.

PRESIDENT: Is the club satisfied with Article IV un-
                    changed?

                    (*Amendments may be proposed from the
                    floor and passed or defeated. If there is no
                    discussion of the article or if no changes are
                    voted, the article in its original form is con-
                    sidered approved.*)

                    (*All succeeding articles with the proposed
                    changes are considered in their turn. The
                    proposed changes are approved or modified
                    or rejected; or substitute changes are pro-
                    posed from the floor and approved or reject-
                    ed by vote of the club; or the original article
                    is retained unchanged. New articles or sec-
                    tions or paragraphs may be moved and ap-
                    proved or modified or rejected. Then, the
                    report having been finished . . .*)

*Amendments
proposed
from the
floor*

MR. L: MR. President, I move the adoption of this
                    report as amended.

MR. H: I second the motion.

PRESIDENT: It has been moved by MR. L and seconded
                    by MR. H that the report of the committee
                    on revision of the Bylaws be adopted as
                    amended. Are you ready to vote?

*Motion to
adopt the
amended
Bylaws*

MANY: Question.

PRESIDENT: The question will be put. All those in favor
                    of adopting the report will say "aye." (*They
                    vote.*) All those who are not in favor will
                    say "no." (*They vote.*) The motion is car-
                    ried and the revision of the Bylaws is adopt-
                    ed. The Chair instructs the Secretary to see
                    that the revised Bylaws are printed in proper
                    form and made available to the members of
                    the club.

MR. L: MR. President.

PRESIDENT: MR. L.

MR. L: I move that the committee appointed to re-
                    vise the Bylaws be now discharged.

MR. R: I second the motion.

PRESIDENT: Shall the committee on revision of the By-laws be now discharged? Is there any discussion? (*Pause.*) If not, all those in favor will stand. (*They stand and are counted.*) Those opposed will now stand. (*They stand and are counted.*) There being a ⅔ majority in favor, the motion is carried, and the committee is discharged.

Committee is discharged by a ⅔ vote

Are there any other reports of special committees to be made at this time? (*Since there apparently are none, . . .*)

The next order of business is Unfinished Business. Is there any unfinished business that should be brought before the club at this time?

Unfinished business

MR. G: MR. President.

PRESIDENT: MR. G.

MR. G: At the last meeting I made a motion that the club authorize the purchase of a new filing cabinet for the office of the club. After prolonged discussion, the motion was tabled with a primary and a secondary amendment adhering to it. I now move that the motion be taken from the table.

To take a motion from the table

MR. M: I second the motion.

PRESIDENT: You have heard the motion. It is not debatable. All those in favor of taking MR. G's former motion from the table will say "aye." (*They vote.*) Those who are opposed will say "no." (*They vote.*) There being a majority in favor, the motion is carried. Therefore MR. G's motion made at the last previous meeting that the club authorize the purchase of a new filing cabinet for the office of the club is now before you. There were two amendments adhering to it when it was tabled. The question first is on the secondary amendment, which was proposed by MR. E, that the words "unless approved by the Executive Committee" be added to the primary amendment, which provided that the cost

Amendments adhering to the tabled motion

was not to exceed $75. Do you wish to discuss the motion to amend the amendment?

SOMEONE: Question.

PRESIDENT: Are you ready for the question. (*Pause.*) If so, all in favor will say "aye." (*They vote.*) All those opposed will say "no." (*They vote.*) The motion is carried.

The question now is on the primary amendment as amended. It reads thus: "that the original motion be amended by adding the words *at a cost not to exceed $75, unless approved by the Executive Committee.*" Do you wish to discuss the motion? (*Discussion follows. When it lags—*) Are you ready for the question?

SEVERAL: Question.

PRESIDENT: The question has been called for. All those in favor will say "aye." (*They vote.*) Those opposed will say "no." (*They vote.*) The motion is carried.

The question now is on the original motion by MR. G, "that the club authorize the purchase of a new filing cabinet for the office of the club," modified by the amendments just adopted. Do you wish to discuss the original motion further?

MR. G: Question.

PRESIDENT: Are you ready for the question? (*Pause.*) If so, all those in favor of the original motion as amended will say "aye." (*They vote.*) Those who are opposed will say "no." (*They vote.*) The motion is carried, and a new filing cabinet will be purchased. The chairman of the Board of Trustees will take note.

Is there any further unfinished business to be brought up at this meeting? (*Pause.*) If not, we shall pass to the head of New Business.   *New business*

According to the revised Bylaws now in force, a nominating committee of five members must be appointed at this meeting to   *Revised Bylaws now in force* draw up a full slate of candidates for the annual election of officers, which will take place at the next meeting one month from today. Accordingly, the Chair appoints on the Nominating Committee MR. S, MR. D, MR. U, MR. X, and MR. C. MR. S will be the chairman of the committee.

Chairman appointed first

Is there any other new business that should be considered now?

MR. S: MR. President.

PRESIDENT: MR. S.

MR. S: The main staircase of the clubhouse is in great need of repairs, as every member is aware. I think it would be dangerous to neglect it longer. Therefore I move that bids for making the necessary repairs be secured at once.

MR. J: I second the motion.

PRESIDENT: It is moved and seconded that bids be secured at once for repairing the main staircase of the clubhouse. Do you wish to discuss the motion?

MR. M: MR. President.

PRESIDENT: MR. M.

MR. M: I move that the question be postponed until the next regular business meeting and that it be made a special order.

To postpone and make a special order

MR. V: I second the motion.

PRESIDENT: It has been moved by MR. M and seconded by MR. V that . . . (*repeats the motion*). Do you wish to discuss the motion? (*Discussion follows. Then—*) If there is no further discussion, the question will be put. (*Pause.*) A ⅔ majority is necessary to pass this motion. All those in favor of the motion will please stand. (*They are counted.*) Those opposed will stand. (*They are counted.*) The motion is carried.

A ⅔ vote needed

MR. F: MR. President.

PRESIDENT: MR. F.

MR. F:	There are two bills now pending in the state legislature which, if passed, will have a detrimental effect on the welfare of this club. They are House Bill — and House Bill —. (*He explains the bills and the effect that they will have.*) I move that a committee of three members be appointed by the Chair to confer at once with the representative of this district and oppose these bills.
MR. R:	I second the motion.
PRESIDENT:	It has been moved by MR. F and seconded by MR. R that . . . (*repeats the motion*). Do you wish to discuss the motion? (*Discussion follows. Then—*) Are you ready for the question?
SEVERAL:	Question.
PRESIDENT:	The question is called for. All those in favor of the motion will say "aye." (*They vote.*) Those opposed will say "no." (*There are no answers.*) The motion is carried unanimously. The Chair appoints MR. F, MR. R, and MR. D. MR. F will be the chairman of the committee. Is there any further new business?
MR. J:	MR. President.
PRESIDENT:	MR. J.
MR. J:	We have long been in need of a regular conference or committee room where committees could meet and work without disturbance. I believe that Room No. — would be suitable for such purposes. The cost of decorating would be small, and the only furniture needed would be a long table and a number of chairs. Therefore I move that Room No. — be decorated and furnished as a permanent conference room.
MR. K:	I second the motion.
PRESIDENT:	You have heard the motion. Do you wish to discuss it?
MR. O:	MR. President.
PRESIDENT:	MR. O.

To appoint a special committee

The chairman is named first

MR. O:	Back here in the rear of the hall we could not hear the number of the room.	*Remarks should be audible to all*
PRESIDENT:	The room in question is No. —. (*Discussion follows*. Then—)	
MR. S:	MR. President.	
PRESIDENT:	MR. S.	
MR. S:	Since it is getting late, I move to adjourn.	
MR. V:	I second the motion.	
PRESIDENT:	You have heard the motion to adjourn. As many as are in favor of the motion will say "aye." (*They vote*.) Those who are opposed will say "no." (*They vote*.) There being a majority in favor, the motion is carried. The meeting is adjourned. (*He raps the desk with the gavel and leaves the chair*.)	*"To adjourn" unqualified*

Fifth Model Meeting—(One Month Later)

(*The following items comprise the agenda of this meeting*)

1. Roll-call.
2. Reading of minutes of the last previous meeting.
3. Secretary's report.
4. Reports of the other officers (president's report is last).
5. Reports of boards and standing committees:
   a. Executive Committee.
   b. Board of Trustees.
   c. Finance Committee.
   d. Public Relations Committee.
   e. Program Committee.
   f. Membership Committee.
6. Reports of special committees:
   a. Committee on Legislation.
   b. Nominating Committee.
7. Special Orders:
   Question of getting bids on repairing stairs.
8. Unfinished Business:
   Question of decorating and furnishing Room No. — as a permanent committee or conference room.
9. General Orders:
   Election of officers for the coming year.
10. New Business.
11. Adjournment.

*(The chairman has the typewritten Order of Business
on the desk before him.)*

PRESIDENT: *(Tapping desk with a gavel.)* The meeting
will come to order. The Secretary will call
the roll.

Call to order

SECRETARY: *(Seated at his desk, calls the roll. After com-
pleting the first roll-call, he reads again the
names of those who did not respond to the
first call, in order to avoid error and to record
the presence of those who may have arrived
after the first reading of the names.)*

*First and
second
roll-calls*

PRESIDENT: The Secretary will now read the minutes of
the last previous meeting.

*Reading of
minutes*

SECRETARY: *(Standing, reads the minutes.)*

PRESIDENT: Are there any corrections or additions to the
minutes? *(Pause.)* If not, they stand approved as read. We shall now hear the Secretary's annual report.

*Minutes
approved
by general
consent*

SECRETARY: *(Stands and reads his report.)*

PRESIDENT: What shall be done with this report?

*Report of
secretary*

MR. C: MR. President.

PRESIDENT: MR. C.

MR. C: I move that the report be accepted.

MR. D: I second the motion.

PRESIDENT: Will you discuss the motion? *(Pause.)* If not,
the question will be put. *(Pause.)* All those
in favor will say "aye." *(They vote.)* All
those opposed will say "no." *(They vote.)*
The motion is carried. *(The reports of the
other officers are called for and handled in
the same manner.)*

*Reports
of other
officers*

The next order of business is the reports of
boards and standing committees. The Chair
will report for the Executive Committee. *(He
gives his report of business transacted at
meetings of the committee. Then—)* Are
there any questions or comments? *(Pause.)*
If not, the committee will assume that the
report is approved. *(He gives a typewritten
copy to the Secretary.)*

*Report
of Executive
Committee*

We shall proceed to the report of the Board

of Trustees. The Chair calls on MR. R, who is chairman of the Board.

MR. R: MR. President, the Board of Trustees wishes to present the following report. (*He reads the report and delivers a typewritten copy to the Secretary.*)

Report of Board of Trustees

PRESIDENT: What shall be done with this report?

MR. K: MR. President.

PRESIDENT: MR. K.

MR. K: I move to accept the report.

MR. V: I second the motion.

PRESIDENT: Is there any discussion of the motion to accept the report? (*Discussion follows.*)

SEVERAL: Question.

PRESIDENT: The question is called for. (*Pause.*) All those in favor of the motion will say "aye." (*They vote.*) All those opposed will say "no." (*They vote.*) The motion is carried.

The next report will be that of the Finance Committee.

MR. B: MR. President.

PRESIDENT: MR. B, chairman of the Finance Committee.

MR. B: (*Reads his report and delivers a typewritten copy to the Secretary.*)

Report of Finance Committee

PRESIDENT: You have heard the report of the Finance Committee. What do you wish to do with it? (*The procedure in considering and disposing of the report is the same as above. Next, the reports of the Public Relations Committee and the Program Committee are called for, given, and considered in the same manner. Then—*)

The report of the Membership Committee is next. The Chair calls on MR. F, the chairman of the Membership Committee.

MR. F: MR. President, we are pleased to report that, pursuant to the instructions of the club to make a special effort to add 150 new members to our club, we have been very successful to date. I have here the applications of 50 responsible and prominent men who wish to be admitted. I will read the names now, MR. Chairman, if the club is ready to vote on them.

PRESIDENT: Proceed with the reading.

MR. F: (*Reads the names*) I move that these men be admitted into membership.

MR. W: I second the motion.

PRESIDENT: You have heard the motion to admit these men as members. Do you wish to discuss the motion? (*He pauses, but no one rises to speak. Then—*) If not, ballots will be distributed, and the candidates will be voted on individually, as required by our Bylaws. (*He appoints tellers, orders the ballot box to be put in place, and then—*) There will be a brief recess until the voting is completed and the tellers are ready to report.

(*Mimeographed ballots, listing all candidates, are distributed by the tellers. Each member marks his ballot, folds it, and puts it in the ballot box. The tellers, having counted the ballots, deliver their report to the chairman, who announces the outcome of the voting as follows.*)

Candidates for membership are voted on by ballot

The vote shows that all candidates have been elected. The Secretary will notify the candidates that they have been accepted by the club and that they will become active members upon payment of the initiation fee and the current dues.

We now pass to the reports of special committees. First may we have a report from the special legislative committee that was appointed at the last meeting to confer with our representative from this district and oppose House Bills — and —, now pending in the State legislature. The Chair calls on MR. F, the chairman of that committee.

Reports of special committees

MR. F: MR. President, the committee has met twice to formulate plans and has conferred twice by telephone with our representative concerning H.B. — and H.B. —. Since the results of our telephone conversations were not altogether satisfactory to us, we have arranged to go to the capital tomorrow for personal conferences with our representatives and to make other contacts that we think may be helpful. We have no definite results to report as yet.

PRESIDENT: Are there any questions or comments on the report? (*Pause.*) If not, it is approved. We shall next hear the report of the Nominating Committee.

Report approved by general consent

MR. V: MR. President, I rise to a request for information.

PRESIDENT: The member may state his request.

MR. V: Will the election of officers be held immediately after this report is read? (*He remains standing.*)

PRESIDENT: No. The report will be read now, but the election will come under the head of General Orders, which follows Unfinished Business.

MR. V: Then I move, MR. President, that the usual order of business be suspended and that the report of the Nominating Committee be presented under General Orders so that it will immediately precede the election.

Suspending order of business

MR. M: I second the motion.

PRESIDENT: You have heard the motion. A ⅔ majority is necessary to pass it. All those in favor of the motion will stand. (*They are counted.*) Those who are opposed will stand. (*They are counted.*) There being a ⅔ majority in favor, the motion is carried.

We pass now to head of Special Orders. By action of the club at the last meeting, the question of getting bids on repairing the main stairs of the clubhouse was made a special order for this meeting. The motion was made by MR. S and seconded by MR. J. Discussion of that motion is now in order. (*Discussion follows. Then—*) If there is no further discussion, the question will be put. (*Pause.*)

Special orders

All who are in favor of the motion will say "aye." (*They vote.*) Those who are opposed will say "no." (*They vote.*) The motion is carried. The chairman of the Board of Trustees will see that the order is carried out.

Since there are no other special orders, we pass to Unfinished Business. At the last session you were discussing the matter of decorating and furnishing Room No. — as a room for conferences and committee meetings. A motion had been made by MR. J and seconded by MR. K, but the discussion was interrupted by adjournment. The motion is now before you. What shall be done with it? (*Discussion follows. Then*—) Are you ready for the question?

Unfinished business

SEVERAL: Question.

PRESIDENT: The question is called for. All those in favor of the motion will say "aye." (*They vote.*) All those opposed will say "no." (*They vote.*) The motion is carried. If there is no instruction to the contrary, we shall assume that this work is to be arranged for by the Board of Trustees. (*Pause.*) Will MR. R, the chairman of the Board, please take note.

Is there any further unfinished business to be brought up? (*Pause.*) If not, we shall next hear the report of the Nominating Committee. The chairman of the committee is MR. S.

MR. S: MR. President.

PRESIDENT: MR. S.

MR. S: The Nominating Committee recommends the following candidates for the offices to be filled. (*He reads the list.*) The committee has provided mimeographed copies of this report in the form of a ballot containing the names of all nominees on one sheet. There are also blank spaces for nominations from the floor, if there should be such nominations. A second sheet contains the qualifications of the candidates listed. With the permission of the

Report of Nominating Committee

	Chair, we will distribute these two sheets.	
PRESIDENT:	Permission is granted.	
	(*The committee distributes the ballots. When*	*Ballots*
	sufficient time has been allowed for the study	*distributed*
	of the ballot, the Chair raps for order and—)	
	The first office to be filled is that of Presi-	
	dent of the club. In accordance with the	
	Bylaws, two names are offered by the com-	
	mittee. Are there any nominations from the	
	floor?	

MR. R: ⎫		
MR. Q: ⎬	MR. President.	
MR. V: ⎭		
PRESIDENT:	The Chair recognizes MR. R.	
MR. R:	I nominate MR. A for the office of President.	*Nominations*
PRESIDENT:	MR. A has been nominated.	*from the floor*
MR. O:	MR. President.	
PRESIDENT:	MR. O.	
MR. O:	I nominate MR. D.	
PRESIDENT:	MR. D has been nominated.	
MR. Q:	MR. President.	
PRESIDENT:	MR. Q.	
MR. Q:	I move that the nominations be closed.	
MR. G:	I second the motion.	
PRESIDENT:	It has been moved to close the nominations.	*To close*
	This motion is not debatable, and a ⅔ ma-	*nominations*
	jority is required to pass it. All who are in	*for president*
	favor of closing the nominations for Presi-	
	dent will please stand. (*They are counted.*)	
	Those who are opposed will stand. (*They are*	
	counted.) There being a ⅔ majority in favor,	
	the motion is carried. The candidates for	
	President are the two recommended by the	
	committee, viz., MR. F and MR. M, plus the	
	two who were nominated from the floor, viz.,	
	MR. A and MR. D. The mimeographed ballot	
	contains blank lines for the names offered	
	from the floor.	
	The next office to be filled is that of Vice	
	President. There are two names already on	
	the ballot. Do you wish to nominate other	

	candidates? (*Pause.*) The Chair hears no further nominations.
	Next is the office of Secretary. Do you wish to add any names to the two already listed on the ballot?
MR. F:	MR. President.
PRESIDENT:	MR. F.
MR. F:	I nominate MR. K for the office of Secretary.
PRESIDENT:	MR. K has been nominated. Are there others?
MR. M:	MR. President.
PRESIDENT:	MR. M.
MR. M:	I nominate MR. E.
PRESIDENT:	MR. E has been nominated.
MR. V:	MR. President.
PRESIDENT:	MR. V.
MR. V:	I nominate MR. T.
PRESIDENT:	MR. T has been nominated. Are there any other nominations? (*Pause.*) If not, you may add these names to the ballot. There are now five candidates for the office of Secretary: viz., MR. J and MR. R, nominated by the committee, plus MR. K, MR. E, and MR. T, nominated from the floor.
	The next office to be filled is that of Treasurer. The committee candidates are MR. Y and MR. P. Do you wish to nominate others?
MR. W:	MR. President.
PRESIDENT:	MR. W.
MR. W:	Our present treasurer, MR. Z, has held office for only one term and is therefore eligible for reelection, according to our Bylaws. MR. Z, as you all know, has performed the duties of his office most successfully. (*Etc.*) Therefore I nominate MR. Z for the office of Treasurer.
PRESIDENT:	MR. Z has been nominated.
MR. Z:	MR. President.
PRESIDENT:	MR. Z.
MR. Z:	Since my business is demanding more and more attention, I do not believe that I could spare the time needed to perform in an acceptable manner the duties of the Treasurer

Nominations from the floor

Nominations closed

Nomination from the floor

for the coming year. Therefore I request that
my name be withdrawn.

PRESIDENT: If there is no objection, MR. Z's name will   *Nomination*
be withdrawn. Are there any other nomina-   *withdrawn*
tions from the floor? (*Pause.*)

If not, nominations are open for the Board
of Trustees. Five are to be elected, the one
receiving the largest number of votes to be
the chairman of the Board. The ballot contains the names of ten candidates. Do you
wish to nominate others? (*Pause.*)

If not, we shall proceed to the nomination
of candidates for the Membership Committee. Five members are to be elected, the one
receiving the most votes to be the chairman of the committee. Ten names are listed
on the ballot. Do you wish to add others?
(*Pause.*)

If not, (*etc., as before, for the remaining
offices. Then, when all nominations are in—*)

The Chair declares all nominations to be now   *Nominations*
closed. Members will please mark their bal-   *declared*
lots and deposit them in the ballot boxes. The   *closed*
Chair appoints MESSRS. I, N, L, and W as   *Tellers*
tellers to count the ballots. MR. I will be   *appointed*
chairman of the tellers.

If there is no objection, there will be an intermission of ten minutes, or until the tellers   *Intermission*
are ready to report. (*He taps the desk with*   *by general*
the gavel and steps down from the floor.)   *consent*

(*Intermission*)

PRESIDENT: (*Having returned to his place, taps desk with*   *Reassembling*
gavel.) The meeting will come to order. Are
the tellers ready to report?

MR. I: MR. President.

PRESIDENT: MR. I.

MR. I: The result of the balloting is as follows: (*He*   *Tellers' report*
reads the list of candidates, giving the num-
ber of votes received by each and hands the
report to the President. Then—)

PRESIDENT: The balloting shows a clear majority for

MR. F, who is therefore elected President; for MR. O, who is therefore elected Vice President; for MR. Y, who is therefore elected Treasurer. The following candidates for the Board of Trustees each received a majority of the votes (*He reads the names*). Therefore they are elected. MR. L, having received the largest number of votes, will be the chairman of the Board, in accordance with our Bylaws. The following candidates for the Membership Committee each received a majority . . . . (*He reads the list. He then reports the results of the balloting for any other offices that were to be filled. Then finally*—).

Election results announced by Chair

The contest for the office of Secretary was not decided, since no one of the candidates received a majority of the votes cast. It will be necessary to take a second ballot for this office. Therefore will MR. I see that new ballots are distributed.

One contest undecided

MR. H: MR. President.
PRESIDENT: MR. H.
MR. H: I move that the two candidates who received the smallest number of ballots for Secretary be dropped from the list.

MR. O: I second the motion.
PRESIDENT: It has been moved that the two candidates who received the smallest number of votes be dropped from the list. The motion is not debatable. All who are in favor will say "aye." (*They vote.*) All who are opposed will say "no." (*They vote.*) The motion is carried. Accordingly the names of Mr. —— and Mr. ——, which have the smallest number of votes, will be dropped.

Dropping the lowest

(*He waits, seated, while the ballots are being distributed and until the members have had time to mark their ballots. Then, standing*—) Will the tellers please collect the ballots, tally them, and report the result.

Reballoting

(*He sits down and waits until the ballots are collected and the tellers have withdrawn to count them. Then, standing—*)

While the ballots are being counted, we shall proceed to the head of New Business, if there is no objection. Is there any new business that should be brought up at this meeting?

(*Consideration of new business gets under way. Then, 10–15 minutes later, when there is an opportunity to get the floor—*)

New business

MR. I: MR. President.

PRESIDENT: MR. I.

MR. I: The tellers are ready to report.

PRESIDENT: If there is no objection, we shall hear the report now.

MR. I: The result of the reballoting for the office of Secretary was as follows (*He reads the names of the candidates and the number of votes received by each. He then delivers to the President a copy of the ballot containing the complete tally for each office and each candidate. This report is signed by all the tellers.*)

Interruption for tellers' report

PRESIDENT: The reballoting shows a clear majority for MR. R as Secretary. MR. R is therefore elected. The election is now complete.

We shall resume the discussion of new business. Is there any further new business to be considered at this meeting? (*The discussion of new business is resumed from the point at which it was interrupted by the report of the tellers.*)

New business resumed

MR. V: MR. President.

PRESIDENT: MR. V.

MR. V: I wish to present the following resolution: "Whereas the Superintendent of Schools of this city has . . . .
. . . .
. . . . and
"Whereas the result of that act has been . . . .
. . . .

Resolution presented

"Therefore be it resolved that this club goes on record as being opposed to said act and all similar acts of political discrimination in the management of the public schools."

I move that this resolution be adopted.

MR. S: I second the motion.

PRESIDENT: You have heard the resolution and the motion to adopt it. Do you wish to discuss the motion?

MR. P: MR. President.

PRESIDENT: MR. P.

MR. P: Although I agree with the spirit of this resolution, I think it would be a mistake to adopt such a statement and make it a matter of public record, for by so doing we would seem to be meddling in affairs with which we, as a club, are not concerned. The successful prosecution of our program necessitates the friendly cooperation of all agencies in the city, even of the agency whose acts this resolution condemns. We cannot afford to jeopardize the friendship of the Superintendent of Schools in this city. Therefore I urge that the motion be defeated.

(*Others get the floor and speak, some in favor of the motion, some against it. Then—*)

MR. D: MR. President, I rise to a point of order.

PRESIDENT: The member may state his point.

MR. D: Is there a quorum now present? If not, it is out of order to vote on this motion.

Question of quorum

PRESIDENT: Will the Secretary and the Sergeant-at-arms please count the members present. (*Sergeant-at-arms reports count to secretary.*)

SECRETARY: MR. President.

PRESIDENT: MR. Secretary.

SECRETARY: There is just a quorum present; i.e., one third of the total membership.

PRESIDENT: Then the point of order is not well taken. Since a quorum is present, we shall proceed with the business in hand. Is there any fur-

ther discussion of the motion to adopt the
resolution offered by Mr. V? (*Pause.*) If not,
the question will be put. All who are in favor
will stand. (*They are counted.*) Those who
are opposed will stand. (*They are counted.*)
The motion is carried and the resolution is
adopted. (Mr. V *delivers a copy of the resolution to the Secretary.*)

*Secretary
receives
copy of
resolution*

MR. P: MR. President.
PRESIDENT: MR. P.
MR. P: I wish to serve notice now that at the next
               meeting I shall move to rescind the action
               just taken.

*Notice
of motion
"to rescind"*

PRESIDENT: The Secretary will record the notice. Is there
               any further business to be presented at this
               meeting?
MR. W: MR. President.
PRESIDENT: MR. W.
MR. W: I move that we adjourn.
MR. G: I second the motion.

*"To adjourn"
unqualified*

PRESIDENT: You have before you a motion to adjourn.
               All who are in favor will say "aye." (*They
               vote.*) Those who are opposed will say "no."
               (*They vote.*) The motion is carried. The
               meeting stands adjourned. (*He taps the desk
               with his gavel and leaves the chair.*)

Sixth Model Meeting

NEW BUSINESS

(*First part of meeting omitted.*)

PRESIDENT: We pass now to the head of New Business.
               Is there any new business to be considered
               at this time?

New business

MR. M: MR. President.
PRESIDENT: MR. M.
MR. M: Our meetings last too long. When an adjourn-
               ment comes at a very late hour, some mem-
               bers are unable to catch the last train home

and must remain in the city overnight. The
only alternative, which is also unsatisfactory,
is to be excused early from the meeting. It
seems to me that the only satisfactory solu-
tion is to have a fixed time for adjournment.
Therefore I move that 10 P.M. be set as the
permanent deadline for adjournment.

MR. H: I second the motion.

PRESIDENT: It has been moved to set 10 P.M. as the per-   *Making*
                manent deadline for adjournment. Is there   *a standing*
                any discussion? (*Discussion follows. There*   *rule*
                is little agreement. Then—)

MR. C: MR. President.

PRESIDENT: MR. C.

MR. C: I move that we go into a Committee of the   *Committee*
                Whole to consider this question.   *of the Whole*

MR. R: I second the motion.

PRESIDENT: You have heard the motion that we go into
                a Committee of the Whole in order to con-
                sider the question. Are there any remarks?
                (*Pause.*) If not, all who are in favor of the
                motion will say "aye." (*They vote.*) All who
                are opposed will say "no." (*They vote.*)
                There being a majority in favor, the motion
                is carried. The Chair will ask MR. O to pre-
                side. (MR. O *comes forward. The President*   *A chairman is*
                leaves the desk.)   *appointed*

[CHAIRMAN: (*Tapping desk with gavel.*) Discussion is
  (MR. O)   now in order on the question of the ten
                o'clock deadline for adjournment.

MR. C: MR. Chairman.

CHAIRMAN: MR. C.

MR. C: (*Expresses his views.*)

MR. R: MR. Chairman.

CHAIRMAN: MR. R.

MR. R: (*Gives his opinions.*)

MR. F: MR. Chairman.

CHAIRMAN: MR. F.

MR. F: (*Expresses his opinion.*)
                (*In this manner each person desiring to speak*
                gets the floor and discusses the motion. Any

member may speak as often as he can get "the floor" if no limits are prescribed by the committee and if "the floor" is not sought by a person who has not spoken before on the question. The only motions in order are "to adopt," "to amend," and "to rise and report." The discussion will end at the time that was set by the club, if any was set, when it passed the motion "to go into a Committee of the Whole." If no time was set by the club, the procedure is as follows:)

MR. P: MR. Chairman.

CHAIRMAN: MR. P.

MR. P: I move that the committee rise and report.   *Motion*

MR. V: I second the motion.   *"to rise and*

CHAIRMAN: You have heard the motion "to rise and re-   *report"*
              port." Do you wish to debate it?

SEVERAL: Question.

CHAIRMAN: All who are in favor will say "aye." (*They vote.*) All who are opposed will say "no." (*They vote.*) The motion is carried.

              (*The President, MR. F, comes forward, receives the gavel from MR. O, and continues*   *The president*
              with New Business from the point where it   *takes charge*
              had been interrupted by the motion "to go   *again*
              into a Committee of the Whole.")

PRESIDENT: Are you ready to vote on the question of a ten o'clock deadline for adjournment?

SEVERAL: Question.

PRESIDENT: The question is called for. All those who are in favor of the motion will say "aye." (*They vote.*) All those who are opposed will say "no." (*They vote.*) The motion is lost. Is   *The vote*
              there any further new business?

MR. E: MR. President.

PRESIDENT: MR. E.

MR. E: I move to amend Standing Rule No. 7 by   *Amending a*
              striking out the words "8 P.M." and substi-   *standing rule*
              tuting the words "7:30 P.M.," so that the rule
              will read as follows: "The meetings of this
              club from June 1 to September 1 shall begin

	at 7:30 and during the remainder of the year at 8:30 P.M." (*He gives reasons.*)	
PRESIDENT:	You have heard the motion. Is there a second? (*Pause.*) If not . . .	
MR. G:	I second the motion.	
PRESIDENT:	It is seconded by MR. G. Do you wish to discuss it? (*Discussion follows. Then—*) Are you ready for the question?	
SEVERAL:	Question.	
PRESIDENT:	Since no previous notice was given, a ⅔ majority is necessary to pass this motion. All those who are in favor of the motion will stand. (*They are counted.*) Those who are opposed will stand. (*They are counted.*) There being a ⅔ majority in favor, the motion is carried.	*See p. 45*

Is there any further new business?

MR. P:	MR. President.	
PRESIDENT:	MR. P.	
MR. P:	I move to rescind the action taken at the last previous meeting on the resolution offered by MR. V. (*He gives reasons.*)	*See p. 162*
MR. D:	I second the motion.	
PRESIDENT:	It has been moved by MR. P and seconded by MR. D to rescind the action taken at the last previous meeting in adopting the resolution offered by MR. V. Do you wish to discuss the motion to rescind? (*Discussion follows. Then—*)	*To rescind*
SOMEONE:	Question.	
PRESIDENT:	If there is no further discussion, the question will be put. (*Pause.*) The Chair reminds you that a ⅔ vote is necessary to pass a motion to rescind. All those who . . .	*The chairman makes an error*
MR. P:	MR. President, I rise to a point of order.	*Question of order*
PRESIDENT:	The member may state the point.	
MR. P:	Only an ordinary majority is necessary to pass a motion to rescind if previous notice has been given. The record will show that I gave notice at the last meeting.	*Previous notice was given (Cf. p. 162)*
PRESIDENT:	(*After consulting the minutes of the last*	

meeting) The point is well taken. The Chair
was in error. All those who are . . .

MR. H: MR. President.

PRESIDENT: MR. H.   *To expunge*

MR. H: I move to amend the motion by adding the   *from the*
            words "and expunge it from the record."   *record*

MR. J: I second the motion to amend.

PRESIDENT: You have heard MR. H's motion to amend by
            adding the words "and expunge it from the
            record." Do you wish to discuss it?
            (*Discussion follows. Then—*)

SEVERAL: Question.

MR. T: MR. President.

PRESIDENT: MR. T.

MR. T: I move that the vote on this question be taken   *"Yeas"*
            by "yeas" and "nays."   *and "nays"*

MR. L: I second the motion.

PRESIDENT: All who favor voting by "yeas" and "nays"
            will say "aye." (*There are few votes.*) Those
            who are opposed will say "no." (*They vote.*)
            The negative vote seems to be unanimous.
            The motion is lost.

            The question now is on MR. H's motion to
            amend the motion "to rescind" by adding
            the words "and expunge it from the record."
            The Chair advises you that, according to
            *Funk & Wagnalls Book of Parliamentary Pro-
            cedure,* by Bridge, the vote required to pass
            this amendment should be a majority of the   *Majority*
            entire membership. All those who favor this   *of entire*
            amendment will stand. (*They are counted.*)   *membership*
            All who are opposed will now stand. (*They   *needed*
            are counted.*) Since there is not a majority
            of the entire membership in favor, the mo-
            tion is lost.

            The question now is on MR. P's motion "to
            rescind." Is there any further discussion of
            that motion? (*Pause.*) If not, all those who
            are in favor will say "aye." (*They vote.*) All
            who are opposed will say "no." (*They vote.*)
            The motion is carried.

Do you wish to present any further new business at this time? (*He waits, but no one rises to address the Chair.*) If not, the Chair declares the meeting adjourned. (*He taps the desk with his gavel and leaves the chair.*)

Chairman adjourns the meeting

CHAPTER XXIV

GUIDE TO SYSTEMATIC STUDY

The number references are to pages.

168

INDEX

References are to pages

172